LETTERS ON THE AUTONOMY PROJECT

BEFORE YOU START TO READ THIS BOOK, take this moment to think about making a donation to punctum books, an independent non-profit press,

@ https://punctumbooks.com/support/

If you're reading the e-book, you can click on the image below to go directly to our donations site. Any amount, no matter the size, is appreciated and will help us to keep our ship of fools afloat. Contributions from dedicated readers will also help us to keep our commons open and to cultivate new work that can't find a welcoming port elsewhere. Our adventure is not possible without your support.

Vive la Open Access.

Fig. 1. Detail from Hieronymus Bosch, *Ship of Fools* (1490–1500)

LETTERS ON THE AUTONOMY PROJECT. Copyright © 2022 by Janet Sarbanes. This work carries a Creative Commons BY-NC-SA 4.0 International license, which means that you are free to copy and redistribute the material in any medium or format, and you may also remix, transform and build upon the material, as long as you clearly attribute the work to the authors (but not in a way that suggests the authors or punctum books endorses you and your work), you do not use this work for commercial gain in any form whatsoever, and that for any remixing and transformation, you distribute your rebuild under the same license. http://creativecommons.org/licenses/by-nc-sa/4.0/

First published in 2022 by dead letter office, BABEL Working Group, an imprint of punctum books, Earth, Milky Way.
https://punctumbooks.com

The BABEL Working Group is a collective and desiring-assemblage of scholar-gypsies with no leaders or followers, no top and no bottom, and only a middle. BABEL roams and stalks the ruins of the post-historical university as a multiplicity, a pack, looking for other roaming packs with which to cohabit and build temporary shelters for intellectual vagabonds. We also take in strays.

ISBN-13: 978-1-68571-042-2 (print)
ISBN-13: 978-1-68571-043-9 (ePDF)

DOI: 10.53288/0358.1.00

LCCN: 2022939551
Library of Congress Cataloging Data is available from the Library of Congress

Book design: Vincent W.J. van Gerven Oei
Cover design: Janet Sarbanes

spontaneous acts of scholarly combustion

HIC SVNT MONSTRA

LETTERS ON THE AUTONOMY PROJECT

JANET SARBANES

(p.)

Contents

FIRST LETTER
This Book Is for You · 15

SECOND LETTER
Autonomy as Our Project: Thoughts of and on Castoriadis · 19

THIRD LETTER
On Castoriadis's Critiques of Capitalism, Marxism, and Liberal Democracy · 29

FOURTH LETTER
On the Autonomy Project in My Life and Lifetime · 37

FIFTH LETTER
On Difference, Self-Valorization, and the Unexpected Subject · 43

SIXTH LETTER
On Black Autonomisms of the Sixties and Seventies · 51

SEVENTH LETTER
Creation Time: On Black Cultural Nationalism and the Black Arts Movement · 59

EIGHTH LETTER
On the Fourth of July in Los Angeles · 69

NINTH LETTER
Dear Teddy, Dear Herbert: On the Autonomy of Theory and of the University · 75

TENTH LETTER
On Art's Autonomy, Frankfurt School-Style · 83

ELEVENTH LETTER
On Being Apart Together and Being Together Apart · 91

TWELFTH LETTER
On Art, Affect, and Occupy · 101

THIRTEENTH LETTER
On Autonomy and Emplacement · 111

FOURTEENTH LETTER
On New Forms of Autonomous Politics in Our Era and a New Mode of Instituting · 119

FIFTEENTH LETTER
On Communization and/as Autonomy · 127

SIXTEENTH LETTER
On the Autonomy Project in Art Today, Which Is Everywhere and Nowhere · 135

SEVENTEENTH LETTER
Autonomy, Meet Autonomy: On Art, Gentrification, and Refusal · 145

EIGHTEENTH LETTER
On Educating for Autonomy and the Early Years of CalArts · 157

LAST LETTER
Not an End But a Beginning · 169

Bibliography · 175

Acknowledgments

I'm profoundly grateful for all the love that went into this labor. Heartfelt thanks to Ken Ehrlich and Lena Sarbanes Ehrlich, who buoyed me with their care and humor, especially during lockdown. And for our ongoing conversation around art and politics, Ken – this book would not exist without it. To the Sarbanes, Pappas and Moochnek-Ehrlich families, as always; and to the Gang of Ten, formerly known as the NELA Babysitting Co-op. To my colleagues and friends at and from CalArts, with special gratitude for the support and encouragement of Tisa Bryant, Gabrielle Civil, Andrew Culp, Brian Evenson, Douglas Kearney, Michael Leong, Maggie Nelson, Anthony McCann, Lee Anne Schmitt and Allison Yasukawa. To Tracy McNulty and Brad Zukovic for the desert residencies. To CalArts MA Aesthetics and Politics Director Arne de Boever, who invited me to teach APA (Art, Politics, Autonomy) in the early stages of this project, and to my MA and MFA students for their engagement and enthusiasm.

Thank you to my generous and patient editor at punctum books, Vincent W.J. van Gerven Oei, and to Jason E. Smith, who gave of his time and insight as an early reader. Thanks also to James Warren, whose keen eye helped me ready the manuscript for submission. And to punctum books and CalArts for supporting my book and open access publishing writ large. I'm grateful for the Andy Warhol/Creative Capital Foundation Art Writers Grant, which kickstarted this whole project.

Thank you to the various autonomous collectives in LA that have given me sustenance and hope: Machine Project, Human Resources, The Poetic Research Bureau, The Public School, Critical Resistance Los Angeles, Chuco's Justice Center, the L.A. Tenants Union, and the Feminist Center for Creative Work among them. And finally, thank you in memoriam to my parents Paul and Christine Sarbanes, for showing me that the struggle for a better world is in fact the stuff of life.

FIRST LETTER

This Book Is for You

If you've picked up a book of letters on the autonomy project, you're likely to be an artist, activist, or academic (and if you're not, please read along, because there's sure to be something in here for you too). If you're an artist, perhaps you've long struggled with the notion that a separate sphere exists for art and that only by keeping to this sphere can art be said to be political, through its difference from all other discourses. Though this otherness of art is famously articulated as an otherness to capitalism, you've actually observed that the opposite is more often true — that today, at least, art and capitalism seem united in their purpose and organization. You ask yourself the relevant questions: Is it possible to be political and still be an artist? Or to be an artist and still be political? You're attentive to the social dimensions of art's making, reception and affects — you think part of the answer may lie there. Whatever your practice, you aren't content to let the socio-historical moment just pass you by. This book is for you.

If you're an activist, you're likely to be the kind of activist who has a commitment to spontaneity, solidarity, affects, and tactics. That doesn't mean you don't also have a commitment to analysis, strategy, and planning, but you know that's not the whole picture, as much as it claims to be. There has to be a spark. Because you believe there has to be a spark, you're open to the possibilities of where that spark might come from. And you may be familiar with other political and aesthetic traditions besides the European ones, with their narrow fixation on the avant-garde — traditions in which experiments with forms of expression and forms of life are practiced by everyone. This book is for you too.

If you're an academic (and you may be all three of these things, or none of them), you're not a gatekeeper; in fact, you struggle to keep the gates open. You believe the classroom is a place unto itself, but you also believe anyone should be able to access that place without ransoming their lives. You may also have ransomed your own life to be there, and you know that isn't the way it should be. You may feel the university is bankrupt in its current incarnation — your university may *be* bankrupt — and you want to make and do something else in its place. *Study,* some call it, others, *autonomy*. This book is also for you.

Where possible and relevant in these letters I will draw on other letters, to keep us in the epistolary register, where people are more likely to say what they feel and think as they are first feeling and thinking it — before they've decided what's possible or impossible. This is an undisciplined space. You will find familiar critics and theorists here, but you will also find ways of thinking and writing about art that are not art history or art criticism and ways of thinking and writing about politics that are not political science or political theory. The epistolary form — its brevity, urgency, modesty, and provisionality — will keep us in the realm of becoming, potentiality, and the lucid dream. In particular, the *open* letter (both the ones I write to you and the ones I cite) seems like the right form for speaking of autonomy, because it articulates not only an *I* and a *you* but a *we*.

One of the central aims of this book is to think through and recalibrate the relationship between art and politics by way of autonomy. Indeed, I believe we cannot face our current crisis of social imagination and political will without a better understanding of autonomy both as a concept and a practice. But just as importantly, this book was conceived in a moment of struggle, and it seeks to contribute to that struggle. Whatever the context of its reading, that is the context of its writing — this is a work of praxis. Some of these letters explore political and aesthetic theories of autonomy; others hearken back to the reignition of the radical social imaginary in the late sixties and early seventies, with special attention paid to Black Radical, Feminist, and Autonomist Marxist approaches to liberation; still others discuss the re-emergence of the radical imaginary in our own time, proof that another world is possible, dear A, every minute of every day.

SECOND LETTER

Autonomy as Our Project: Thoughts of and on Castoriadis

Dear A,

Why should we interest ourselves in autonomy? Why should it become — or is it already — our project? And what exactly do I mean by autonomy? I'm decidedly not working with the notion of personal autonomy, which emphasizes the primacy of the individual as lone decision maker and actor, and is rationalistic and legalistic in orientation. This is the understanding of autonomy that undergirds the political theory of "possessive individualism," as critiqued by C.B. MacPherson, according to which people are said to own themselves and their skills, which they then sell on the open market.[1] What I'm talking about has more in common with the concept of "relational autonomy" put forward by feminist philosophers, which, while upholding individual agency (in particular, women's agency), acknowledges interdependence.[2] But the definition of autonomy I'm most interested in differs from both of these in its focus on autonomy

---

[1] C.B. MacPherson, *The Political Theory of Possessive Individualism: Hobbes to Locke* (Oxford: Oxford University Press, 2011).

[2] See Catriona MacKenzie and Natalie Stoljar, eds., *Relational Autonomy: Feminist Perspectives on Autonomy, Agency and the Social Self* (Oxford: Oxford University Press, 2000).

as the realm of psychic and social *creativity*, the source of new forms, both aesthetic and political, and its understanding of the relation between individual and collective as something generative and mutualistic, not limiting and antagonistic.

I owe this way of thinking to the work of Greek theorist Cornelius Castoriadis, who defines autonomy not as "a watertight frontier against everything else" but as a mutually constitutive relationship between individual and collective.[3] A psychoanalyst by training, Castoriadis grounded his notion of the individual in the individual *psyche*, which while admittedly covered and thoroughly penetrated by its "social armor," is nonetheless able to draw on the unconscious for new meanings.[4] But the radical imagination to which the individual psyche has access can only take on meaning for others in an autonomous society that is profoundly aware of the fact that history and society are themselves *ongoing creations,* emerging out of a "permanent welling of representations, desires and affects."[5] Only under these circumstances can the individual psyche "find or create the social means of publicly expressing itself in an original manner and contribute perceptibly to the self-alteration of the social world."[6] Castoriadis thus insists on always using the phrasing "individual-and-collective autonomy," because one cannot exist without the other.

The political and social form that corresponds most to individual-and-collective autonomy, he argues, is that of radical democracy, which is based on the ongoing questioning of existing institutions by the *dēmos,* or people, and the refashioning of those institutions "not once and for all, but continuously."[7] In a

---

[3] Cornelius Castoriadis, "An Interview," *Radical Philosophy* 56 (Autumn 1990): 35.

[4] Cornelius Castoriadis, "Power, Politics, Autonomy," in *Philosophy, Politics, Autonomy: Essays in Political Philosophy,* ed. David Ames Curtis (New York: Oxford University Press, 1991), 146.

[5] Ibid.

[6] Ibid.

[7] Cornelius Castoriadis, *Political and Social Writings, Vol. 1: 1946–1955: From the Critique of Bureaucracy to the Positive Content of Socialism,* ed.

radical democracy, "questions of freedom, of justice, of eq and of equality [can] always be posed anew within the fram. work of the 'normal' functioning of society."[8] Castoriadis argues that this situation appeared strongly in the case of the Ancient Greek *polis,* a direct democracy (at least for male slaveholders), and weakly in the case of modern democratic republics. And here it's important to note that radical democracy, as Castoriadis articulates the concept, corresponds only in part to what we understand by "direct democracy." For radical democracy denotes not only full participation in collective decision-making (as opposed to representative government) but a society permeated with a sense of its own self-instituting and attentive to the emergence of new forms.

Weak or strong, he cautions us, autonomous societies remain the historical exception. Most societies tend instead toward heteronomy and the assertion of hierarchy, authority, and conformity, to a greater or lesser degree, imputing their origins to external authorities such as God, Nature, Capitalism, and so forth (he returns to the Greek etymology of the words to clarify this point: *autos*/self and *nomos*/law, versus *heteros*/other and *nomos*/law). Every society has its core meanings, or in Castoriadis's words, "social imaginary significations," through which

> the total world given to a particular society is grasped in a way that is determined practically, affectively and mentally, that an articulated meaning is imposed on it, that distinctions are made concerning what does or does not possess value (in all the senses of the word "value," from the strictly

and trans. David Ames Curtis (Minneapolis: University of Minnesota Press, 1988), 31.

8 Cornelius Castoriadis, "The Greek and the Modern Political Imaginary," in *World in Fragments: Writings on Politics, Society, Psychoanalysis, and the Imagination,* ed. and trans. David Ames Curtis (Stanford: Stanford University Press, 1997), 87.

economic to the strictly speculative), and what should and should not be done.[9]

But the core meanings of a heteronomous society are never challenged. Heteronomous societies are closed societies with fixed institutions, in which "the closure of signification shuts off in advance not only every political question as well as every philosophical one, but equally every ethical or aesthetic question."[10]

Insofar as it can be weakened or strengthened, then, autonomy becomes for Castoriadis a *project*: the political project of "collective emancipatory movement" toward radical democracy and an autonomous society and the intellectual project of "self-reflecting, uninhibitedly critical thought."[11] It also becomes, in equal measure, a project for art. Not surprisingly, Castoriadis's orientation toward creativity as the wellspring of social organization shifts our focus away from laws and onto *forms*. Indeed, he explicitly redefines *nomos* as form: "We conceive of autonomy as the capacity, of a society or of an individual, to act deliberately and explicitly in order to modify its law — that is to say, its form."[12] New forms of politics, thought, and signification all contribute to the project of autonomy, but within this constellation, Castoriadis singles art out for special mention, since it engages most directly with both the flux of meaning *and* the psyche's radical imagination, giving form to "the Chaos [both] of what is, and that within man himself."[13]

Art, and more specifically modern art, he argues, engages simultaneously in "the exploration of ever new strata of the

---

9 Cornelius Castoriadis, *The Imaginary Institution of Society* (Cambridge: MIT Press, 1998), 146.
10 Cornelius Castoriadis, "Culture in a Democratic Society," in *The Castoriadis Reader*, ed. and trans. David Ames Curtis (Oxford: Blackwell, 1997), 341.
11 Cornelius Castoriadis, "Radical Imagination and the Social Instituting Imaginary," in *The Castoriadis Reader*, 337.
12 Cornelius Castoriadis, "Physis and Autonomy," in *World in Fragments*, 340.
13 Cornelius Castoriadis, "Culture in a Democratic Society," 343.

psyche and the social," mirroring in microcosm the workings of autonomous societies at large.[14] Indeed, it is able to exist "only by questioning meaning as it [is] each time established and by creating other forms for it."[15] If the revolutionary project for Castoriadis is the reorganization and reorientation of society toward radical democracy by means of autonomous action, then art offers up both a praxis and a horizon for that undertaking.

Hang on, you say, if Castoriadis is such an important thinker, then why have I never heard of him? And what's a letter without a little gossip? Castoriadis certainly dishes it up in his 1986 essay "The Movements of the Sixties," where he pointedly argues that the autonomy project, which he saw briefly manifested in the French student occupations and worker strikes of May 1968 and in sixties liberation movements all over the globe, was in essence betrayed by the school of "68 thought" that followed:

> It is strange to hear people label today "68 Thought" a set of authors who saw their fashionableness increase after the failure of May '68 and of the other movements of the time and who did not play any role even in the vaguest sense of a "sociological" preparation of the movement, both because their ideas were totally unknown to the participants and because these ideas were diametrically opposed to the participants' implicit and explicit aspirations.[16]

Castoriadis roundly condemns thinkers like Lacan and Foucault, as well as the theories of structuralism and poststructuralism they espoused, for insisting upon "man's impotence before his own creations."[17]

Indeed, he locates the beginning of the end of politics in this "effacement of the subject,"[18] by which he means structuralism's

---

14 Ibid., 345.
15 Ibid.
16 Cornelius Castoriadis, "The Movements of the Sixties," in *World in Fragments*, 50.
17 Ibid., 54.
18 Ibid., 51.

replacement of actors with systems, an effacement that poststructuralism perpetuated even as it hunted for the ghost in the meaning-making machine. And he suggests that all of this so-called '68 thought actually profited from the *failure* of the sixties liberation movements, legitimating their limits by arguing that because "politics aims at the whole, it is therefore totalitarian."[19] In so doing, structuralist and poststructuralist theorists provided justification from the seventies onward for the "incipient privatization" of tens or even hundreds of thousands of erstwhile movement participants, while "at the same time [managing] to jump on the bandwagon of a vague sort of 'subversion.'"[20]

Castoriadis playfully suggests that *real* "68 thought" — that is, the thought that truly belongs to the movement — can be found not only in anthologies of writing by its participants but in the various collections of "wall writings" or graffiti that appeared during university occupations. In these "texts," which we might also look upon as letters to passersby, "what constantly appears is criticism of the established order, the famous appeals to the imagination (one wonders how that could relate to Foucault, Derrida, Bourdieu, or even Lacan!) and obviously the celebration of freedom and of 'jouissance,' but above all of socialism and of a new social order."[21] Castoriadis is trash talking here ("if 30,000 copies of Lacan's *Ecrits* were sold before '68, 300,000 would be sold after"), and we must acknowledge that what he considers to be authentic '68 thought bears a striking resemblance to his own, but to be fair, the group and journal *Socialisme ou Barbarie,* which he cofounded with Claude Lefort, was a major influence on the movement. Student leader Daniel Cohn-Bendit and his older brother Gabriel have acknowledged this,[22] and the Situationist International, a revolutionary group of artists responsible for much of the May '68 graffiti, owed the

---

19 Ibid., 53.
20 Ibid.
21 Ibid., 52.
22 Daniel Cohn-Bendit and Gabriel Cohn-Bendit, *Obsolete Communism: The Left-Wing Alternative,* trans. Arnold Pomerans (London: André Deutsch, 1968), 18.

better part of their analysis up to that point to Castoriadis (the SI's leader, Guy Debord, was also a member of *Socialisme ou Barbarie*).[23]

And anyway, Castoriadis's main point holds true: that the "linguistic turn" in critical theory post '68 tended to emphasize the flux of meaning *in opposition to* — though ostensibly *in preparation for* — political action.[24] Grant Kester has leveled a similar criticism at the art theory of the seventies and eighties — a period in which conceptions of visual art also came to be dominated by the poststructuralist paradigm. According to Kester, this orientation produced among academics and artists

> an extreme skepticism about organized political action and a hypervigilance regarding the dangers of co-option and compromise entailed by such action, the ethical normalization of desire and somatic or sensual experience, and the recoding of political transformation into a form of ontic disruption directed at any coherent system of belief, agency or identity.[25]

This approach was taken up by artists as well, so that the artwork itself came to be defined as a subversive text that would "trigger

---

23 See Stephen Hastings-King, "L'Internationale Situationniste, Socialisme ou Barbarie, and the Crisis of the Marxist Imaginary," *SubStance* 28, no. 3, issue 90, special issue: "Guy Debord," eds. Pierpaolo Antonello and Olga Vasile (1999): 26–54.

24 Two popular May '68 thinkers whose work has much in common with Castoriadis are Gilles Deleuze and Félix Guattari. All three share an interest in radical creativity, a distrust of the psychoanalytic formulation of subjectivity in terms of a negative experience of lack, and a commitment to thinking through the political and philosophical effects of May '68. Most significantly, Deleuze and Guattari do not fall prey to the individualism-recast-as-subversion that Castoriadis condemns here. Given their seeming affinities, it seems odd that he wouldn't include the two of them in this essay, even to stipulate his differences with their work, which have largely to do with the self-reflexive nature of autonomy as he conceives it — the element of awareness it requires — versus the liberation of libidinous drives championed by Deleuze and Guattari.

25 Grant Kester, *The One and the Many: Contemporary Collaborative Art in a Global Setting* (Durham: Duke University Press, 2011), 54.

a cascading series of insights into the contingency of all forms of coherent meaning."[26]

In contrast to Kester's more nuanced analysis, the popular critique of poststructuralism is strictly authoritarian. Our social meanings and values are *not* contingent, that argument goes, they're eternal and unchanging. But from the point of view of Castoriadis, it's not that we've gone too far in destabilizing meaning, it's that we haven't gone far *enough*, haven't attended to the new forms and significations which the flux of meaning, and our awareness of that flux, enable. Autonomy is "not just the unlimited self-questioning about the law and its foundations," he insists, "it is also, in light of this interrogation, to make, to do and to institute."[27]

Castoriadis goes on to draw a clear distinction between what he calls the dimensions of "instituted" and "instituting" society. One is born into a society that is already instituted, meaning whose horizon of possibility is seemingly already given. But in fact, the horizon of possibility is never fixed since new institutions are constantly forming — specific institutions within society *and* the institution of society as a whole. Castoriadis defines the word "institution" broadly, to mean "norms, values, language, tools, procedures and methods of dealing with things and doing things, and, of course, the individual itself, both in general and in the particular type and form (and their differentiations: e.g., man/woman) given to it by the society considered."[28] In an autonomous society, or at least a society moving toward and not away from autonomy, we are attuned to this power of making, though it's important to note that Castoriadis's focus is not so much on specific institutions themselves but the possibility of "a new *mode* of instituting and a new relation of society and of individuals to the institution."[29]

---

26 Ibid., 50.
27 Castoriadis, "Power, Politics, Autonomy," 164.
28 Cornelius Castoriadis, "The Imaginary: Creation in the Socio-Historical Domain," in *World in Fragments*, 6.
29 Castoriadis, *Imaginary Institution of Society*, 363.

How does Castoriadis evaluate May '68 and the other radical movements of the sixties? He doesn't try to argue that they succeeded in their goals, acknowledging the "immense difficulty involved in prolonging in a positive direction the critique of the existing order of things."[30] But he does insist they were necessary, that liberation movements are always necessary, and that they have real effects. While admitting that the failure of the autonomy project has been with us since the beginning of modern times, he notes it very rarely is total: "In most cases these movements result in the formal institution of certain rights, freedoms, guarantees under which we still live. In other cases, nothing is formally instituted, but deep traces are left in the mental outlook and actual life of societies."[31] It's okay to acknowledge this continued failure, he argues, but it's not okay to forget that

> thanks to and by means of the type of collective mobilizations represented by the movements of the sixties, [...] [contemporary] societies find sedimented within themselves the institutions and characteristics that, somehow or other, make them viable, and may one day serve as the starting point and the springboard for something else.[32]

In "Movements of the Sixties," Castoriadis asks us to remember him, a '68 thinker eclipsed by his peers. But he also asks us to remember ourselves as creative agents within history, our individual-and-collective autonomy the potential source of hitherto unseen forms of social and political creativity. This is "the meaning of 1776 and 1789, of 1871, of 1917 and May '68," he reminds us, a meaning that lies "in the attempt to bring into being other possibilities for human existence."[33]

---

30 Castoriadis, "Movement of the Sixties," 55.
31 Ibid.
32 Ibid., 56.
33 Ibid.

TAKE YOUR DREAMS FOR REALITY
FORM DREAM COMMITTEES
POWER TO THE IMAGINATION[34]

---

[34] Examples of May '68 graffiti.

THIRD LETTER

On Castoriadis's Critiques of Capitalism, Marxism, and Liberal Democracy

Dear A,

Have I neglected to spell out how the autonomy project is anticapitalist? Be assured that it is, and profoundly so, but by way of a trenchant critique of Marxism. Castoriadis grounds his anticapitalism in a historical phenomenon that preceded Marx, the workers' movement of 1790–1840, which met the rise of industrial capitalism with fierce resistance, first in England and then on the European continent. It deserves our attention, he argues, because it sought not merely to better the conditions of workers in the factory but to counteract the capitalist imaginary *in its entirety*. The fact that the birth of capitalism wasn't able to transform society into "one huge factory, with a single command structure and a single logic," had a lot to do with the workers' self-organization. All of the "relevant ideas," Castoriadis insists, were formulated during this period *before* Marx: "the fact of exploitation and its conditions, the project of a radical transformation of society, that of a government by the producers and for the producers, the abolition of the wage system."[1]

But when Marx reinterprets all of human history as resulting from the evolution of the forces of production, Castoriadis argues, he paradoxically *reproduces* the logic of capitalism and becomes "the principal theoretician and artisan of the penetration into the workers and socialist movement of ideas which made technique, production and the economy into the central factors," rather than the workers' own political activity.[2] While conceding that Marx "undoubtedly aided people enormously to believe — and therefore, to struggle," Castoriadis suggests that he ultimately succumbed to the fantasy of total mastery inherited from capitalism, offering up a "salvation guaranteed, in the last analysis, by something much greater than the fragile and uncertain activities of human beings, namely, the 'laws of history.'"[3]

Castoriadis strenuously objects to this closure of meaning, which he says in his own life and thinking forced him to choose between "remaining Marxist and remaining revolutionary."[4] "Politics," he argues, "is neither the concretization of an Absolute Knowledge nor a technique; neither is it the blind will of no one knows what. It belongs to another domain, that of making/doing, and to the specific mode of making/doing that is praxis."[5] He defines praxis as conscious but not entirely conscious activity, or "lucidity without total elucidation," insisting that because the goal of praxis is the new, it "cannot be reduced to the simply

---

[1] Cornelius Castoriadis, "The Only Way to Find Out If You Can Swim Is to Get into the Water: An Introductory Interview," in *The Castoriadis Reader*, ed. and trans. David Ames Curtis (Oxford: Blackwell, 1997), 26.

[2] Cornelius Castoriadis, "The Pulverization of Marxism-Leninism," in *World in Fragments: Writings on Politics, Society, Psychoanalysis, and the Imagination*, ed. and trans. David Ames Curtis (Stanford: Stanford University Press, 1997), 62.

[3] Ibid., 63.

[4] Ibid., 14.

[5] Cornelius Castoriadis, "Marxism and Revolutionary Theory: Excerpts," in *The Castoriadis Reader*, 150.

materialized tracing of a pre-constituted rational order."[6] In this way, Castoriadis's theory of politics opens out onto aesthetics: "To do something, to write a book, to make a child, a revolution, or just making or doing as such, is projecting oneself into a future situation which is opened up on all sides to the unknown, which, therefore, one cannot possess beforehand in thought."[7] At the same time, we must still take into consideration the social whole — praxis must *face* the totality, encountering it as an "*open-ended unity in the process of making itself.*"[8]

Castoriadis's decisive break with historical materialism took place in the context of rapid postwar growth and redistributive economic policies that dramatically improved the living conditions of the working class, undercutting the argument that the contradiction of capitalism was the sole driver of history. But he was no fan of what he called "bureaucratic capitalism," which merely replaced private *owners* of capital as the main antagonists of workers with a stratum of state, private, and union *managers*. He perceived a similar situation developing in postwar communist countries, where a new ruling class privately if collectively owned and controlled production — and went so far as to label this another, more total, indeed totalitarian, form of bureaucratic capitalism. In both instances, the system functioned in the interest of a small minority at the top, a stratum of directors or "order-givers" devoted to "production for production's sake." Laboring people, the "order-takers," would "not be able to free themselves from oppression, from alienation, and from exploitation unless they [overthrew] this system by eliminating hierarchy and by instaurating their collective and egalitarian management of production."[9]

It was in this context that Castoriadis arrived at the notion of a socialism rooted in worker self-organization, which he would subsequently fold into the concept of autonomy, expanding his

---

6   Ibid., 151.
7   Ibid., 162.
8   Ibid., 164. Emphasis in the original.
9   Cornelius Castoriadis, "Recommencing the Revolution," in *The Castoriadis Reader*, 121.

horizon from the self-management of production to the self-management of society. He was well aware that this set the stage for new political actors. As David Ames Curtis notes,

> by the very early sixties, he recognized that the shop stewards' movement in England, the nascent youth, women's and antiwar movements, and the struggles of racial and cultural minorities offered prospects for revolt against modern society that might give rise to unpredictable and unprecedented expressions of autonomy.[10]

This awareness is one of the things that makes Castoriadis's thought useful to us today in theorizing new forms of struggle and new ways of relating to and across those struggles.

Though harsh, his critique of Marxism is an immanent one — one might say he's reading the Marx of the *Eighteenth Brumaire*, who insists that we make our own history, though not under circumstances of our own choosing, against the Marx of *A Contribution to the Critique of Political Economy* and ultimately, *Capital*. As Castoriadis himself claims:

> Our revision consists of making more explicit and precise what was the genuine, initial intention of Marxism and what has always been the deepest content of working-class struggles — whether at their dramatic and culminating moments or in the anonymity of working-class life in the factory. [...] Socialism aims at giving a meaning to people's life and work; at enabling their freedom, their creativity, and the most positive aspects of their personality to flourish; at creating organic links between the individual and those around him, and between the group and society; at reconciling people with themselves and with nature.[11]

---

10 David Ames Curtis, "Cornelius Castoriadis: An Obituary," *Salmagundi* 118/119 (Spring–Summer 1998): 56.

11 Cornelius Castoriadis, "On the Content of Socialism II," in *The Castoriadis Reader*, 50.

As Brian Singer observes, where Marx issued an "economic critique of the political," Castoriadis gives us a "political critique of the economic."[12] He does so by continually challenging the core meanings, or "social imaginary significations," of capitalist society. Two of those core meanings are economy and the economic, "central social imaginary significations which do not 'refer' to something but on the basis of which a host of things are socially represented, reflected, acted upon and made as economic."[13] Another related meaning is the premise that we are always and everywhere economically motivated — "that the true nature of man is to be a reproductive-economic animal."[14] A third core meaning is temporal. In a capitalist society, we are organized by capitalist *time*, which is, on the one hand, measurable, homogenous, uniform, and "wholly arithmetizable" and, on the other hand, infinite, "a time of indefinite progress, unlimited growth, accumulation, rationalization."[15] In his later work, Jeremy Smith notes, Castoriadis adds another primary social imaginary signification of capitalism — its "thrust" toward the unlimited extension of rational mastery, "harnessing human creativity to schemes of maximization of output and minimization of cost."[16] These core meanings worked their way into Marxist theory but were contested by the workers' movement that preceded it, and they are further contested by any movement toward autonomy, insofar as it seeks to create new social imaginary significations.

While we're clarifying Castoriadis's politics, we should also clarify his attitude toward democracy. The radical democracy aimed at by the autonomy project is not to be confused with liberal democracy as it exists today. In his aptly titled essay collection *The Rising Tide of Insignificancy*, Castoriadis argues that

---

12 Brian Singer, "The Early Castoriadis: Socialism, Barbarism and the Bureaucratic Thread," *Canadian Journal of Political and Social Theory* 3, no. 3 (1979): 39.
13 Castoriadis, *Imaginary Institution of Society*, 362.
14 Ibid., 28.
15 Ibid., 207.
16 Jeremy C.A. Smith, "Capitalism," in *Cornelius Castoriadis: Key Concepts*, ed. Suzi Adams (London: Bloomsbury, 2014), 163.

contemporary Western society has taken the form of a "liberal oligarchy," peddling an emptied-out version of democracy, where the emphasis is entirely on procedure as opposed to the political activity of the *dēmos,* and in which an "ultrathin stratum of society" dominates and governs. "Of course, it is liberal," he says. "It is open (more or less), and it gets itself ratified every four, five, or seven years by a popular vote."[17] But it has very little to do with autonomy. "If the governing part of this oligarchy goes too far afield," he observes, "it will get itself replaced — by the other part of the oligarchy, which has become more and more like it." Indeed, Castoriadis expresses skepticism that liberal societies even have a fundamental interest in democracy: "Could [liberal society] accommodate itself to a true democracy, to effective and active participation of citizens in public affairs? Do not present-day political institutions also have as their goal to distance citizens from public affairs and to persuade them that they are incapable of concerning themselves with these matters?"[18]

At the same time, he pulls back from the Marxist argument that the rights and liberties guaranteed by liberal democracy are merely formal, a ruse by bourgeois revolutions to stave off truly radical democracy in the interest of capitalism. Rather, he argues, they emerged out of "people's centuries-old struggles," and this is the source of their strength — for wherever these rights and liberties have merely been imported, "they have always been almost lackluster as well as fragile."[19] It makes more sense, he suggests, to think of them not as *formal* but as *partial*: "The exercise of the right to assemble, for instance, or to seek redress of grievances, or publish a newspaper or a book, can have important effects on our social and political life."[20] But

---

17 Cornelius Castoriadis, "The Idea of Revolution (1989)," in *The Rising Tide of Insignificancy (The Big Sleep),* trans. and ed. anonymously as a public service (n.p.: Not Bored, [2003]), 303, http://www.notbored.org/RTI.pdf.
18 Ibid.
19 Cornelius Castoriadis, "Democracy as Procedure, Democracy as Regime," in *The Rising Tide of Insignificancy,* 351.
20 Ibid.

the existence of these rights does not in and of itself constitute democracy, and so "a major part of the struggle for democracy is aimed at instaurating real conditions that would permit everyone effectively to exercise these rights."[21] This, too, is a return to the early spirit of Marx and Engels, who criticized bourgeois democracy, not because it was democratic, but because it was bourgeois.[22]

Perhaps Castoriadis's most trenchant criticism of liberal democracy — which is all the more relevant to its current, neoliberal incarnation — has to do with its hypostatization of the individual. Though committed to individual autonomy, in the context of liberal democracy he finds it to be hypervalued, because the creation of meaning by each individual for their life is not inscribed within the framework of a *collective* creation of significations. Championing individual autonomy in the context of an otherwise heteronomous society, where social meanings are pregiven, amounts to a mere "empty" individualism, such that

> in the contemporary West, the free, sovereign, autarchic, substantial "individual" is hardly anything more, in the great majority of cases, than a marionette spasmodically performing the gestures the social-historical field imposes upon it: that is to say, making money, consuming, and "enjoying" (if that happens to occur).[23]

The individual gives to their life only that "meaning" that has currency under capitalism, "the non-sense of indefinite increases in the level of consumption."[24]

---

21 Ibid., 352.
22 Michael Harrington, "Marxism and Democracy," *Praxis International* 1, no. 1 (April 1981), available online at *Palinurus: Engaging Political Philosophy*, https://anselmocarranco.tripod.com/id25.html.
23 Cornelius Castoriadis, "The Dilapidation of the West," in *The Rising Tide of Insignificancy*, 79–80.
24 Ibid., 80.

By contrast, the autonomy project seeks to push beyond the hyperindividualism and procedural limits imposed by liberal democracy to affirm unlimited inquiry and continuous creation as principles of social organization. It rejects both the capture of the creative impulse by the capitalist imaginary, and the devaluation of that impulse (the "fragile and uncertain activities of human beings") by historical materialism. While emerging from the workers' struggle, autonomous thought can account for radical movements beyond that struggle, because it encompasses and attributes meaning to new forms that don't conform to capitalist imaginary significations of the political or the economic. And it takes seriously — in a social sense — acts of creation in other arenas (art, science, technology, etc.), because it sees them as stemming from — and contributing to — the questioning of all pregiven meanings that radical democracy requires. It brings into view the double reality of alienation and creative struggle, instituted and instituting society, and helps us to identify and support autonomous activity in the here and now. In comparison to the international proletarian revolution — or the universal rights of man — the scale of this undertaking may feel unbearably small. But when understood as the striving for individual-and-collective autonomy across every sphere and institution of society, its horizon expands exponentially, further than the eye can see.

FOURTH LETTER

On the Autonomy Project in My Life and Lifetime

Dear People's Free Community Health Clinic
Dear People's Food Co-op
Dear New Era Bookstore
Dear Baltimore Branch of the Black Panther Party
Dear S.O.U.L School
Dear Liberation House Press
Dear Black Book
Dear Mother Rescuers from Poverty
Dear 31st Street Bookstore for Women and Children
Dear Diana Press
Dear Women's Growth Center
Dear *Women: A Journal of Liberation*
Dear Pratt Street Conspiracy
Dear Jonah House
Dear Viva House
Dear Ida Braiman Collective
Dear John Brown Collective
Dear Club Charles
Dear Marble Bar

Dear A,

I could've made this whole book about Castoriadis. He means that much to me, and certainly his thought is worthy of closer attention and deeper analysis than I've performed here. But instead I want to undertake a praxis inspired by his work, in the interest of struggle and of understanding why people struggle, and what art might have to do with all of that. I want to take a moment first, though, to position myself as the writer of these letters, one to whom the autonomy project speaks especially loud and clear.

Growing up in 1970s Baltimore, I could feel autonomy all around me. A newly abandoned city, bankrupted by white flight and fragmented by redlining and urban renewal, Baltimore was a prime location for organizing outside of and beyond electoral politics. It was home to all of the projects listed above, "dear" now in that they're mostly gone, dear at the time because they helped feed the radical social imaginary: political organizations, bookstores, presses and journals dedicated to Black Power, feminist, anti-poverty, housing rights, and antiwar activism; communal housing and workers collectives; punk bars. Autonomy was there in the language, too, since our words, norms, laws, and conceptual apparatuses are also institutions. "The People" (as opposed to "the American People," or "the Public") was still the subject of history, and poverty was a problem to be solved collectively, not a personal sin to confess.

Children of what were then called "good white liberals," my brothers and I lived in a white, upper-middle-class neighborhood but attended Mt. Royal #66, an elementary–middle school that had been the first in Baltimore to integrate and whose student body was now majority black and working class or poor. The administration and teachers were for the most part Black women, which in and of itself was an inversion of the power structures I'd already come to know, and though not as radical as the nearby S.O.U.L. School Institute associated with the Black Panther Party, Mt. Royal centered Black history, culture, and solidarity throughout the curriculum and the culture of the school. Celebrations of Kwanzaa, Martin Luther King Jr. Day assemblies (before the national holiday was created), the formal teaching of the Black National Anthem, and the informal teaching of Stevie Wonder's version of the birthday song (also an ode to MLK), a first grade teacher rumored to be a Panther — all of it hinted at a social imaginary beyond what I'd previously encountered or even thought possible. This wasn't the multicultural education of the nineties, which replaced the coercive "American melting pot" metaphor with a "patchwork quilt" of difference that covered up inequities rather than contesting them. This was still education for liberation, my first exposure to the autonomy project. Learning the words to Funkadelic's "One Nation under a Groove" and "Grooveallegiance" from my friends on the playground, I pledged my earnest (if irrelevant) commitment to an autonomous collectivity-in-formation, fictive and real at the same time ("one nation and we're on the move / nothing can stop us now").

I'm certain my investment in political autonomy/ies is partially a response to this early exposure to the radical valorization of Black life, which called into question the structures of race and class I'd already absorbed and profited from and would continue to absorb and profit from. But it no doubt also stems from the jarring juxtaposition of that experience with another one: my father's rapid rise in electoral politics, as he ran successfully for the U.S. House of Representatives in 1970 and six years later for the Senate, the son of Greek immigrants taking on millionaire incumbents with a grassroots "From the People / For the People" campaign. In the wake of the many political and social upheavals of the sixties and early seventies, these two forms of politics didn't seem quite so far apart then as they would a mere decade later, yet it was still clear to me, even as a child, that the power of radical creativity lay with autonomy.

The representative structures of liberal democracy simply paled (figuratively and literally) when compared to a politics that was not just *for* the people but *by* the people. I could see some crossover, notably during my father's election campaigns, when over the course of a long, hot Baltimore summer, an economically and racially diverse, largely female community of volunteers would form, motivated by specific issues and a general desire for change. But after the election, that ad-hoc community evanesced, and the activity of shared social creation was channeled into representation, with power vested in the newly elected official (my dad), and him alone. It was this closing down of possibility, of the forms politics could take, of the kinds of people who are allowed to participate in the ongoing creation of society — this heteronomy — that seemed so at odds with the lessons I'd absorbed at school.

Of course, the expansive political horizon of the revolutionary sixties would soon narrow even more dramatically. Autonomous politics in the U.S. didn't end with Ronald Reagan's election, and heteronomy didn't simply reinstate itself. Richard Nixon had already sailed into office on a wave of authoritarianism twelve years earlier, and as governor of California, Reagan himself had lambasted Berkeley professors for allowing "young people to think they had the right to choose the laws they would obey."[1] The autonomy project *didn't* end in 1980 (the autonomy project never ends), but it ceased to have a hold on the social imagination in its entirety. The revolution that didn't happen was recast as the revolution that *couldn't* happen, with Reagan's British counterpart, Margaret Thatcher, triumphantly proclaiming "no alternative" to capitalism.

As a college student in the late eighties, I joined "Take Back the Night" marches and sit-ins on behalf of the Third World Center on my campus, but how or even if these efforts connected up to a larger radical imaginary was unclear (the Third World Center, named in 1971 to express solidarity with Third World liberation movements, would be rebranded the Center for Equality and Cultural Understanding in 2002). This is not to downplay the powerful organizing that took place throughout the eighties against U.S. imperialism in Central America, support of apartheid in South Africa, and failure to address the

---

[1] "Reagan Interview in Sacramento, Part II," *KQED News*, January 16, 1969, available at San Francisco State University, Academic Technology Archives, Diva, 17:45, https://diva.sfsu.edu/collections/sfbatv/bundles/187218.

AIDS crisis at home, nor any of the other ways in which people continued on with the autonomy project during these years with courage and imagination. It's only to say that this all took place within a horizon of possibility brutally foreshortened by the authoritarian turn.

With the nineties came the long sleep of neoliberalism, Fukuyama's perfect marriage of liberal democracy and global capitalism,[2] the decimation of the commons and the privatization of everything, a collective nightmare papered over by individualist fantasy. During these years, through my own practice as a fiction writer and scholar, and in the discourses surrounding contemporary art and experimental writing, I found ways of thinking through and about autonomy in aesthetic terms: worlds within worlds, the endless potential for and of new forms, including forms of coming together to make and receive art that resisted the subordination of the individual to the collective and vice versa. But the question remained: How did or how could any of this connect up to the radical social imaginary?

The radical social imaginary writ large wouldn't reemerge in my lifetime until the 1994 Zapatista revolution in Chiapas, Mexico, followed by the anti-corporate globalization protests of 1999–2003. In the U.S., it wasn't until after the crash of 2008 that the scaling up began in earnest, with the invocation of the 99% and the intent to Occupy Everything, carried out by the various movements of the squares — Sidi Bouzid, Tahrir, Colon, Syntagma, Zuccotti. On the heels of Trayvon Martin's murder, Black Lives Matter struck at the roots of a system grounded in the opposite assumption, and something turned. The authoritarian tide began once more to recede, revealing that what had seemed like islands of autonomy in a sea of heteronomy was in fact an archipelago, magmatic and connected — and that another society, one attuned to its own making, awaited just below the surface.

---

2   Francis Fukuyama, *The End of History and the Last Man* (New York: Free Press, 1992).

Today we face systemic collapse on many fronts: environmental, economic, political, and social. We live at a time when the radical imaginary is once again legible, while at the same time the waters of authoritarianism — not to mention the actual waters — are rising all around us. Of course, it's no coincidence that just as everything is being called into question, there should come an insistence that *nothing* be called into question. But if we now know, or have once again remembered, that we can remake the world we're born into — though never independently of the situation we find ourselves in — can we be so easily stopped? As a child of the seventies, who came to consciousness in a world where the magma of social imaginary significations was still molten, if no longer explosively so, I recognize this long-lost feeling of possibility. It tells me the scaling up of the autonomy project in our moment is far from over.

FIFTH LETTER

On Difference, Self-Valorization, and the Unexpected Subject

Dear A,

My takes on historical instances of autonomy will of necessity be partial, in both senses of the word, limited by this form and my experience and the fundamental impossibility (for any of us) of knowing everything and getting everything in. But while it may not be enough history to convince you, I hope it's enough to make you see the possibilities, in these moments and in similar ones with which you may be more familiar.

At its core, autonomy has a love of difference, since while conceding the extent to which history has already made us, it remains open to that which isn't yet known, said, or envisioned. This was particularly true of the Italian autonomy movement known as Autonomia, one of whose main theorist and actors, Toni Negri, declared in 1977: "I am other, as also is the movement of that collective praxis within which I move. I belong to the *other* movement of the working class."[1] As we've seen in Castoriadis, it is this "other" movement of the working class that

---

1   Toni Negri, "Domination and Sabotage," in *Autonomia: Post-Political Politics,* eds. Sylvère Lotringer and Christian Marazzi (Los Angeles: Semiotext(e), 2007), 63.

anchors the concept of autonomy by centering workers' creative struggle against capitalism, which Negri himself famously referred to as *self-valorization*. Italy in the years 1968–80, years in which Negri headed up first the workerist group Potere Operaio and then the autonomist organization Autonomia Operaia, was a proving ground for autonomy's potential to take the struggle against capital in new directions—precisely by means of this otherness.

To understand what Negri means by self-valorization, we must consider Marx's own concept of valorization. In Marx, valorization is described as the process whereby capital reproduces and expands the class relationship upon which it rests, with ever more going to the capitalist (the "surplus value" produced by workers in excess of their wages and increased control over the means of production) and ever less going to the worker. This arrangement is upheld through the ideology of work, the seductions of consumer society, and an insistence on the totality of capitalism, for even in situations where workers struggle to improve their lot, the horizon of possibilities is still determined by the interests of capital.

By contrast, Negri's understanding of valorization is rooted in the self-recognition of the working class's *collective independence*.[2] Self-valorization rests on needs, demands, and values drawn from working-class experience and composition, which is to say, the *differentness* of working-class constitution. It is through this process of self-valorization that a revaluation of the totality occurs, and workers begin to think, *work is not good, we don't need that new television, another relation to one's own labor is possible!* Working-class self-valorization doesn't participate in the structuring of capital but rather acts as a force of *destructuration*: "The establishment of working class independence takes place first and foremost in its separation. But separation in this instance means breaking the capital relation."[3] Its goal is to transform the nature of work—even to the point

---

2 Ibid., 62.
3 Ibid., 65.

of its total refusal — rather than win adjustments in wages and hours while leaving the class relationship essentially unchanged.

Within this scenario, Negri argues in "Domination and Sabotage," it's not capital that has the momentum, but the workers movement. Capital must continually struggle to reassert its totality (domination) in the face of working-class resistance (sabotage). Negri reads the entire history of capital "as the history of a continuity of operations of self-re-establishment," set in motion by capital and its State to counter this continuous breakdown.[4] Here again, he raises the specter of his (and the worker's) "otherness": "I define myself by separating myself from the totality: I define the totality as other than me — as a net which is cast over the continuity of the historical sabotage that the class operates."[5]

Autonomia's practices of self-valorization in the factories of Northern Italian cities belonging to Lancia, Michelin, and Fiat included work slowages — hiccup and checkerboard strikes — and production sabotage. During the same period — Negri would say in response — the factories were being restructured and decentralized, automated, and robotized, and tens of thousands of industrial workers laid off. This situation led other Autonomia thinkers, such as Mario Tronti, to formulate a new political strategy of "inside and against: to act on the inside of capitalist development, promoting it through the refusal of work (thus bringing about the introduction of new machines and new technologies), but at the same time to remain against capitalism wanting everything from it."[6] Rather than resist automation, or strike for better jobs, autonomist workers rallied instead around the concept of a "social wage" — a minimum wage that would be guaranteed to all social subjects regardless of employment to support social life beyond the factory.

Autonomia's tactics outside of the factory mirrored the work slowages and sabotage of machinery that had taken place

---

[4] Ibid., 63.
[5] Ibid.
[6] Sylvère Lotringer and Christian Marazzi, "The Return of Politics," in *Autonomia*, eds. Lotringer and Marazzi, 18.

within, resituated now in the realm of consumption rather than production. "Self-reduction" of mounting electricity and phone charges and increased bus fares took place throughout the Northern cities and Rome. Rome and Turin were beset by widespread housing occupations, and "proletarian shopping" expeditions, where groups entered supermarkets en masse and insisted on the sale of goods at reduced prices. When Autonomia in its thought and practice moved beyond the factory gates, out into what Tronti termed "the social factory" of a society permeated through and through by capitalism, new groups joined the workers in their actions — notably housewives, students, and artists — and new political formations began to emerge.[7] Though as Benjamin Noys has convincingly argued, Autonomia's embrace of capitalist acceleration had the deleterious effect of disappearing factory labor into capital, it made other forms of labor suddenly more visible.[8]

Sylvia Federici, Mariarosa Della Costa, Bridget Galtier, and Selma James put forward their revolutionary demand of "wages for housework" in 1972, founding an organization by that name that drew attention to the ways in which women's unwaged labor served the interests of capital. But they were careful to stipulate that this was only an opening salvo:

> To say that we want money for housework is the first step towards refusing to do it, because the demand for a wage makes our work visible, which is the most indispensable condition to begin to struggle against it, both in its immediate aspect as housework and its more insidious character as femininity.[9]

---

7   Stephen Wright, *Storming Heaven: Class Composition and Struggle in Italian Autonomist Marxism* (London: Pluto, 2002), 158.
8   Benjamin Noys, *Malign Velocities* (Winchester: Zero Books, 2014) 46.
9   Sylvia Federici, "Wages against Housework," in *Wages for Housework: The New York Wages for Housework Committee 1972–1973: History, Theory and Documents*, eds. Sylvia Federici and Arlen Austin (Brooklyn: Autonomedia, 2017), 206.

The demand by autonomist feminists for wages for (and against) housework should be understood then not just in terms of actual housework, but as asserting the value of care work – care for husbands/laborers and for children/laborers-to-be that is naturalized and erased by conventional gender role expectations:

> We are housemaids, prostitutes, nurses, shrinks; this is the essence of the "heroic" spouse who is celebrated on "Mother's Day." We say: stop celebrating our exploitation, our supposed heroism. From now on we want money for each moment of it, so that we can refuse some of it and eventually-all-of it.[10]

Wages for Housework also sought an end to women's isolation in the home, issuing a call to collective action: "Nothing can be more effective than to show that our female virtues have a calculable money value, until today only for capital, increased in the measure that we were defeated; from now on against capital for us, in the measure we organise our power."[11] The call for wages was thus a way of articulating a political as well as an economic power — not only the power to strike but also to reorganize society in non-capitalist ways.

The autonomist feminist emphasis on the "otherness" of women's situation under capitalism was in conversation not just with workers' autonomy but with the emerging "sexual difference" strand of Italian feminism, which, as the Milan Women's Bookshop Collective noted, was "not one culturally constructed from biology and imposed as gender, but rather a difference in symbolization, a different production of reference and meaning out of a particular embodied knowledge."[12] In her 1970 essay "Let's Spit on Hegel," Carla Lonzi, a key theorist of sexual difference, argues for a kind of self-valorization when she attacks equality as an organizing principle of liberal feminism:

---

10 Ibid., 207.
11 Ibid.
12 Milan Women's Bookshop Collective, *Sexual Difference: A Theory of Social-Symbolic Practice,* trans. Patrizia Cicogna and Teresa de Lauretis (Bloomington: Indiana University Press, 1990), 27.

> What is meant by woman's equality is usually her right to share in the exercise of power within society, once it is accepted that she is possessed of the same abilities as man. But in these years, women's real experience has brought about a new awareness, setting into motion a process of global devaluation of the male world. [...] Existing as a woman does not imply participation in male power, but calls into question the very concept of power. It is in order to avoid this attack that we are now granted inclusion in the form of equality.[13]

To demand wages for housework, then, was not to ask for equal power with men, but rather to make visible a power differential that could not be ameliorated within the existing society. As Lonzi notes, "We recognize within ourselves the capacity for effecting a complete transformation of life. [...] [W]e are the Unexpected Subject."[14] Her formulation offers up the possibility that, because women's social status hasn't been wholly defined by the wage (if at all, ideologically), they have access to a radical social imaginary both against and *beyond* capitalism, which is in fact what is needed to end capitalism.

Negri himself viewed feminists as the most vibrantly autonomist group on the Italian scene, precisely because of their investment in thinking through difference: "The feminist movement, with its practices of communalism and separatism, its critique of politics and the social articulations of power, its deep distrust of any form of 'general representation' of needs and desires, its love of differences, must be seen as the clearest archetype for this new phase of the movement."[15] Georgy Katsiaficas, a contemporary historian of autonomy, goes a step further, identify-

---

13 Carla Lonzi, "Let's Spit on Hegel," in *Italian Feminist Thought: A Reader*, eds. Paola Bono and Sandra Kemp (London: Basil Blackwell, 1991), 41.
14 Ibid.
15 Quoted in Georgy Katsiaficas, *The Subversion of Politics: European Autonomous Movements and the Decolonization of Everyday Life* (Oakland: AK Press, 2006), 35.

ing feminist currents as "the most significant single source of modern autonomous movements."[16]

Today we can look to the revolutionary autonomous municipalities in the Zapatista-controlled region of Mexico and the Rojava region of Syria for evidence of this fact, which the workerist emphasis of most anti-capitalist organizing (and history of organizing) tends to obscure. In both cases, the dismantling of patriarchal structures has been central to the creation of self-organizing, radically democratic, anti-capitalist, and ecological societies. Rojavan democratic confederalism has its own feminist epistemology, "jinology," which draws on the black intersectional feminist tradition in the U.S. to arrive at an analysis spanning interlocking systems of oppression on the basis of race, ethnicity, class, and gender in the Syrian context.[17] Rojavan feminists have identified strongly with the need "to fight the world," as Michele Wallace put it back in 1977, changing the whole of society rather than just a part of it.[18]

Radical transfeminism — especially where it draws on Marxist thought — has similarly opened up new horizons for the autonomy project, posing a profound challenge to the core capitalist social significations of both labor and gender. It has drawn attention to the labor of gender, which is to say, how gender nonconformity survives in a capitalist context, and the ways in which transgender experiences "straddle the conventional limits of political and private life, workplace and household."[19] And it insists, in the words of Nat Raha, "that another world is necessary — and is already being created — in which trans lives may

---

16 Ibid.
17 Arianne Shahvisi, "Beyond Orientalism: Exploring the Distinctive Feminism of Democratic Confederalism in Rojava," *Sussex Research Online*, http://sro.sussex.ac.uk/id/eprint/80502/.
18 Cited in "The Combahee River Collective Statement (1977)," *Black Past*, https://www.blackpast.org/african-american-history/combahee-river-collective-statement-1977/.
19 See Jules Joanne Gleeson and Elle O'Rourke, "Introduction," in *Transgender Marxism* (London: Pluto, 2021), 2.

flourish."[20] Today, as ever, it is the Unexpected Subject, seeking a complete transformation of life, who continues the questioning of all pre-given meanings that radical democracy requires.

---

20 Nat Raha, "The Limits of Trans Liberalism," *Verso Books* (blog), September 21, 2015, https://www.versobooks.com/blogs/2245-the-limits-of-trans-liberalism-by-nat-raha.

SIXTH LETTER

On Black Autonomisms of the Sixties and Seventies

Dear A,

Not convinced? Need more proof of connection? I don't blame you. When I first started writing these letters, I found myself searching for more explicit linkages between moments of autonomism, hoping to bring to light some hidden correspondence between one movement and another, or even a more "open" one, such as the telegram sent by striking students to striking factory workers in May '68, expressing solidarity "from the occupied Sorbonne to occupied Sud-Aviation." So noticeable in particular seemed the correlations between Autonomia and Black autonomisms of the sixties and seventies, the subject of this letter, that I hoped to find some equally frank communications among them.

I did discover a group *named* Correspondence, which fostered a book collaboration in 1956 between C.L.R. James, Grace Lee Boggs, and Castoriadias titled *Facing Reality*. Both the book, which connected the rise of direct-democratic workers' councils in the Hungarian revolution to pre-Civil Rights struggles for Black autonomy in the U.S., and a subsequent incarnation of Correspondence named after the book, had a documented impact on Black auto workers organizing in Detroit[1] and on Autonomia (for whom *Socialisme ou Barbarie* was also a touchstone).[2] But I'm mindful of what Stefano Harney and Fred Moten, themselves collaborators who hail from both traditions, have to say about looking too hard for intellectual and political *debts,* as opposed to linkages having to do with the content of the thought and action itself. As Moten observes, "I think a whole lot of that work of acknowledging a debt intellectually is really predicated on a notion that somehow the black radical tradition is ennobled when we say that the autonomists picked something up from it."[3] It's a far more autonomist practice to allow for "the possibility of a general movement," in Moten's words, "that then gets fostered when we recognize these two more or less independent irruptions of a certain kind of radical social action and thinking."[4]

So, let's turn our attention now to Black Power and the Black Panthers. Why do I label them autonomisms? Certainly at first glance, the nationalist rhetoric of Black Power and the military stylings of the Panthers seem at odds with the autonomy project, until we consider what it might actually mean to form a nation without land and an army without a nation — what these new forms accomplished with their impossible demands, and how they sparked a reimagining of race, nation, and state. The autonomous dimension of the Black Panther Party for Self-Defense is particularly noteworthy, inasmuch as the Panthers simply refused the laws that were given to them, beginning with their refusal to be policed. Their emphasis on self-defense can be seen as itself a form of self-valorization, which shifted the

---

[1] John H. Bracey, "The Questions We Should Be Asking: Introduction to the 2006 Edition," in C.L.R. James and Grace C. Lee, with Cornelius Castoriadis, *Facing Reality: The New Society: Where to Look for It and How to Bring It Closer* (Chicago: Charles H. Kerr, 2006), 4.

[2] Stephen Wright, *Storming Heaven: Class Composition and Struggle in Italian Autonomist Marxism* (London: Pluto, 2002), 23.

[3] Stefano Harney and Fred Moten, *The Undercommons: Fugitive Planning and Black Study* (New York: Minor Compositions 2013), 153.

[4] Ibid.

locus of violence onto the police themselves, undermining law enforcement claims to "uphold the peace." And the "survival programs" the Panthers created in forty cities around the U.S., offering free breakfast for children, free health clinics, and free clothing, issued a similarly concrete challenge to the capitalist imaginary.

What's more, the Panthers went beyond self-valorization to affirm the autonomous praxis of other liberation movements as necessary to the large-scale project of transvaluation. One example is an open letter that ran in the Black Panther newspaper on August 15, 1970, from Huey Newton to "The Revolutionary Brothers and Sisters," on the subject of the Women's Liberation and Gay Liberation movements, challenging sexism and homophobia among the Panthers as practices that ran counter to the development of a "revolutionary value system":

> Remember, we have not established a revolutionary value system; we are only in the process of establishing it. I do not remember our ever constituting any value that said that a revolutionary must say offensive things towards homosexuals, or that a revolutionary should make sure that women do not speak out about their own particular kind of oppression. As a matter of fact, it is just the opposite: we say that we recognize the women's right to be free. We have not said much about the homosexual at all, but we must relate to the homosexual movement because it is a real thing.[5]

Newton saw in these other movements a liberatory impulse that held revolutionary potential; most importantly, he affirmed their right to be free *in their own way,* while reserving his right to critique actions that ran counter to the Panthers' goal of radically realigning society with the interests of oppressed peoples.[6]

---

5 Huey P. Newton, "The Women's Liberation and Gay Liberation Movements (1970)," *Black Past,* April 17, 2018, https://www.blackpast.org/african-american-history/speeches-african-american-history/huey-p-newton-womens-liberation-and-gay-liberation-movements/.

6 Ibid.

In her 1975 essay "Race, Gender and Class," Selma James notes that one of the major lessons the autonomist feminist movement learned from the black liberation movement was the importance of the relationship between class and caste:

> Those of us in the feminist movement who have torn the final veil away from this international capitalist division of labour to expose women's and children's class position, which was hidden by the particularity of their caste position, learnt a good deal of this from the Black movement.[7]

"Caste" is how James defines collective differences other than class which take on material dimensions and are used as a basis for suppression.[8] Within the Black liberation struggle, she observes, these differences became positively defined as nationalism, with "intellectuals in Harlem" and "Malcolm X, that great revolutionary," both appearing to "place colour above class when the white Left were still chanting variations of 'Black and white unite and fight.'"[9]

Far from a reactionary retreat from class analysis, she contends, "The Black working class were able through this nationalism to *redefine* class," such that "the demands of Blacks and the forms of struggle created by Blacks [became] the most comprehensive working class struggle."[10] Black Liberation "used the 'specificity of its experience' — as a caste and a class both at once — to redefine class and the class struggle itself." This "both at once" resulted in a new revolutionary value system, centered on autonomy, that spanned both class and race (and as articulated in Newton's letter, other differences as well).

---

7 Selma James, *Sex, Race and Class: The Perspective of Winning: A Selection of Writings 1952–2011* (Oakland: PM Press, 2012), 94.

8 James's use of "caste" here, and the use of the term throughout the twentieth century in discussions of race and class, should not be collapsed into the argument on caste presented by Isabel Wilkerson more recently, which draws explicit parallels between "race" in the U.S. and "caste" in India.

9 James, *Sex, Race and Class,* 49.

10 Ibid.

James and her counterparts in Wages for Housework understood that "women and their movement had also to be autonomous of that part of the hierarchy of labor powers which capital used specifically against them. For Blacks it was whites. For women it was men. For Black women it is both."[11] Ultimately, she concludes, "nothing united and revolutionary will be formed until each section of the exploited will have made its own autonomous power felt."[12] In trying to describe the political effects of this autonomous "feeling," she uses the figure of movement, noting that the Black Liberation movement in the United States

> challenged and continues to challenge the most powerful capitalist State in the world. The most powerful at home and abroad. When it burnt down the centres of that metropolis and challenged all constituted authority, it made a way for the rest of the working class everywhere to move in its own specific interests. We women moved.[13]

Stokely Carmichael, soon to become Kwame Ture, uses similar phrasing in his famous "Black Power" speech, delivered at UC Berkeley in 1966, which marked the Student Nonviolent Coordinating Committee's definitive shift away from Civil Rights rhetoric focused on integration. This was partially encapsulated by the younger, more militant organization's substitution of "Black" for "Negro," as a way of flagging a radical new subjectivity in the making. "The institutions that function in this country are clearly racist; they're built upon racism," Carmichael states. "The questions to be dealt with then are: how can black people inside this country move? How can white people who say they're not part of those institutions begin to move?"[14] Carmichael also locates the answer in autonomous practice, advocat-

---

11 Ibid., 97.
12 Ibid.
13 Ibid.
14 Stokely Carmichael, "Black Power (1960)," *Black Past*, July 13, 2010, https://www.blackpast.org/african-american-history/1966-stokely-carmichael-black-power/.

ing for "the right for black people to define themselves as they see fit, and organize themselves as they see fit." He warns: "We don't know whether the white community will allow for that organizing, because once they do they must also allow for the organizing inside their own community. It doesn't make a difference, though — we're going to organize our way."[15]

As James notes, Malcolm X was instrumental in defining Black Power as Black *nationalism,* arguing in his 1963 speech "Message to the Grassroots" that the Black revolution should be based, like all other revolutions, on land: "Land is the basis of all independence. Land is the basis of freedom, justice and equality. [...] A revolutionary wants land so he can set up his own nation, an independent nation."[16] Following in the tradition of the Garveyites and the Nation of Islam, he encouraged Black Americans to separate out from whites, to make their communities self-sufficient, and most importantly, to think of themselves as a nation, on equal stature with other nations around the world, including the nations from which their ancestors had been kidnapped, and the nation in which they now lived. In this way, Black nationalism opened up a new social imaginary, connecting the struggle of Black Americans within the U.S. to national liberation and anti-imperialist struggles in Africa, Asia and Latin America.

The Panthers, while embracing autonomy and Black Power, shied away from nationalism, opting instead for Newton's theory of "revolutionary intercommunalism," which argued that the form of the nation state had been undone by Western imperialism — particularly, and presciently, "corporate imperialism" — such that nationalism was no longer a viable revolutionary strategy. Given that imperialism had spread around the globe, integrating peoples and economies to the point that it was "impossible to 'decolonize,'" Newton asserted the world

---

15 Ibid.
16 Malcolm X, "Message to the Grassroots (1963)," *Black Past,* August 16, 2010, https://www.blackpast.org/african-american-history/speeches-african-american-history/1963-malcolm-x-message-grassroots/.

was now actually a "dispersed collection of communities, existing in a state (abetted by technology) of 'intercommunalism.'"[17] Though currently controlled by a "ruling circle, a small group of people," this collection of communities could be radicalized through alliances:

> If we believe we are brothers with the people of Mozambique, how can we help? They need arms and other material aid. We have no weapons to give. We have no money for materials. Then how do we help? [...] They cannot fight for us. We cannot fight in their place. We can each narrow the territory that our common oppressor occupies. We can liberate ourselves, learning from and teaching each other along the way. But the struggle is the same; the enemy is the same.[18]

While emphasizing the importance of linking up to communities of color around the world, as Malcolm X had done within the paradigm of Black nationalism, Newton saw no need to exclude radical whites from this project. In a 1968 interview with *The Movement Magazine* he affirms Carmichael's invocation of Black Power and his break with the white liberal membership of SNCC, but suggests that in practice this was a reactionary rather than a revolutionary form of politics: "I think that one of SNCC's great problems is that they were controlled by the traditional administrator: the omnipotent administrator, the white person. He was the mind of SNCC."[19] When SNCC committed to black self-determination and turned away from its white liberal members, "it regained its mind, but [...] lost its political perspective."[20]

---

17 Huey P. Newton, "Intercommunalism (1974)," *Viewpoint Magazine,* June 11, 2018, https://www.viewpointmag.com/2018/06/11/intercommunalism-1974/. See also Delio Vasquez's excellent introduction.

18 Huey P. Newton, "Uniting Against a Common Enemy: October 13, 1971," in *The Huey P. Newton Reader,* eds. David Hilliard and Donald Weise (New York: Seven Stories, 2002), 239–40.

19 "SDS: Publication: 'Huey Newton Talks to the Movement,'" Kent State University Libraries, Special Collections and Archives, 8, https://omeka.library.kent.edu/special-collections/items/show/3176.

20 Ibid.

SNCC couldn't or didn't distinguish between the white liberal and the white revolutionary, Newton says, because they were "very much afraid to have any contact whatsoever with white people, even to the point of denying that the white revolutionaries could give support, by supporting the programs of SNCC in the mother country."[21] By contrast, he argues, the Black Panther Party has "NEVER been controlled by white people. The Black Panther Party has always been a black group. We have always had an integration of mind and body. We have never been controlled by whites and therefore we don't fear the white mother country radicals. Our alliance is one of organized black groups with organized white groups."[22]

In its insistence on self-organization as a basis for solidarity with other groups, revolutionary intercommunalism fulfills the promise of revolutionary politics as described by Castoriadis, which is to bring forth "a praxis which takes as its object the organization and orientation of society with a view toward fostering the autonomy of all its members, and which recognizes that this presupposes a radical transformation of society, which will be possible, in turn, only through people's autonomous activity."[23] Or in another, more personal formulation of Castoriadis's: "I want the other to be free, for my freedom begins where the other's freedom begins."[24] The Panthers remain an enduring touchstone for contemporary struggles because they didn't provide a definitive answer as to what liberation looks like but instead insisted that *everybody* grapple with the question.

---

21 Ibid.
22 Ibid.
23 Cornelius Castoriadis, "Marxism and Revolutionary Theory," in *The Castoriadis Reader*, ed. and trans. David Ames Curtis (Oxford: Blackwell, 1997), 152.
24 Ibid., 167.

SEVENTH LETTER

Creation Time: On Black Cultural Nationalism and the Black Arts Movement

Dear A,

Art and aesthetics have been lurking in the background of these letters, but now we must bring them to the fore, because there isn't really a way to understand the Black Power movement without also reflecting on the central roles that Black cultural nationalism and the Black Arts Movement (BAM) played in it.

In their introduction to the Black Arts movement reader *SOS — Calling All Black People*, John H. Bracey Jr., Sonia Sanchez, and James Smethurst single out Malcolm X and John Coltrane as BAM's political and cultural forebears: "Malcolm X had performed the magic that turned 'Negroes' into Black people, but the exact social, political and cultural content of this new self-designation was not self-evident. John Coltrane and the other adherents of what was then called 'free Jazz' demonstrated that one could transgress the boundaries of "western music" and yet create work of great power and beauty."[1] With Coltrane as their model, BAM artists undertook an exploration

---
1   John H. Bracey Jr., Sonia Sanchez, and James Smethurst, "Editors' Introduction," in *SOS–Calling All Black People: A Black Arts Movement Reader*,

"of what it would mean to be liberated, of what it did mean to be Black,"[2] committing themselves to the development of a Black aesthetic or Black aesthetics that "vigorously questioned and challenged white supremacy, the Eurocentric world-view and the literary 'canon.'"[3]

BAM also challenged prevailing notions of the role of art and the artist—that is to say, the very way in which art's autonomy was understood. BAM artists and writers refused to accept a society, in Larry Neal's words, "in which art is one thing and the actions of men another," precisely because they viewed Black Arts as instantiating "the real impulse in back of the Black Power movement, which is the will toward self-determination and nationhood."[4] Yes, art and politics were two different modalities, but in the context of Black autonomy they were engaged in the same project. "A main tenet of Black Power is the necessity for Black people to define the world in their own terms," Neal observes. "The Black artist has made the same point in the context of aesthetics."[5]

The influence of jazz on Black cultural nationalism, both within and without the context of BAM, cannot be overestimated. Ron Karenga, founder of the cultural nationalist organization US, looked to jazz improvisation—the interplay between soloist and ensemble—as a model for the relation between individual and collective, embodying the concept of "diversity in unity or unity in diversity." For Karenga, the individual's role in a jazz ensemble is one expressive of "personality" rather than "individuality," which he perceived as a flawed philosophical and political construct: "Individuality by definition is 'me' in spite of

---

eds. John H. Bracey Jr., Sonia Sanchez, and James Smethurst (Amherst: University of Massachusetts Press, 2014), 2.

[2] Ibid., 5.

[3] Asia Touré, "Poetry and Black Liberations: Freedom's Furious Passions (Reminiscences)," in *SOS–Calling All Black People,* eds. Bracey Jr., Sanchez, and Smethurst, 28.

[4] Larry Neal, "The Black Arts Movement," in *SOS–Calling All Black People,* eds. Bracey Jr., Sanchez, and Smethurst, 57.

[5] Ibid., 55.

everyone, and personality is 'me' in relation to everyone."[6] His critique is reminiscent of Castoriadis's, who you'll remember refused to separate out individual-and-collective-autonomy.

Karenga himself was a controversial figure in the Black Power movement. His organization, US, feuded with the Black Panthers over the direction the movement should take, with US accusing the Panthers of being too closely aligned with white leftist groups, and the Panthers accusing US of depoliticizing the movement with its emphasis on cultural transformation. Toward the end of the sixties, exacerbated by covert FBI operations, their differences deepened into rancor and violence, resulting in the murder of two Los Angeles Panthers, UCLA students John Higgins and Bunchy Carter, by an US member (never convicted) and more retaliatory violence after that.

But the conflict-ridden, COINTELPRO-infiltrated final years of the Black Power movement have clouded our view of its early unity-in-diversity, and the radical imaginary both groups helped to fashion during the period of its greatest activity. While the Panthers rooted their challenge to capitalism and white supremacy in Marxism, Black Power and anti-imperialism, US sought to "ignite Black cultural revolution by introducing an alternative value system, rituals, and aesthetic expression to the broader African American community," drawing selectively on the traditional culture of African communal societies to do so.[7] Karenga's philosophy, Kawaida, from the Swahili word for normal, sought to establish a new, self-valorizing "normal" for Black America, with its roots in African rather than European values and culture. Prefigured by Malcolm Little's assumption of X, the widespread rejection of European names and adoption of African names within and outside of the organization challenged the very institution of naming — and thereby of the social individual — as something given and not made. Perhaps

---

6 Ron Karenga, "Black Cultural Nationalism," in *SOS–Calling All Black People,* eds. Bracey Jr., Sanchez, and Smethurst, 53.

7 Scot Brown, "The US Organization, Maulana Karenga, and Conflict with the Black Panther Party: A Critique of Sectarian Influences on Historical Discourse," *Journal of Black Studies* 28, no. 2 (November 1997): 157.

the best-known alternative cultural practice Karenga and US set into motion was a holiday, Kwanzaa, which is still celebrated by millions in the African diaspora alongside or instead of Christmas. A cultural rather than a religious ritual, Kwanza extols the principles of Umoja (Unity), Kujichagulia (Self-Determination), Ujima (Collective Work and Responsibility), Ujamaa (Cooperative Economics), Nia (Purpose), Kuumba (Creativity), and Imani (Faith).

Though derided by the Panthers, the alternative value system US subscribed to and promoted was certainly perceived as a threat to white supremacy by the FBI, whose report on the organization described the "costume" worn by US members down to the smallest detail: "Besides wearing dark glasses and open sandals, the male members of US wear an allegedly African 'buba,' a three quarter length, loose smock with a modified Mandarin collar." The author of the report dutifully transcribes Karenga's decolonizing rationale for the look: "If you can wear a French beret, a Russian hat, and Italian shoes and not feel funny, you should be able to wear an Afro-American buba."[8] Taken as a whole, the document reveals a clear understanding on the part of the U.S. government that Karenga's version of culture, derived from his studies in anthropology at UCLA, was indeed political in its motives and effects.

Both the Panthers and US were at this time challenging the core social significations of capitalism and white supremacy on a profound level and also creating new ones *ex nihilo* (though as Castoriadis is careful to stipulate, novel creation is always creation *with* something and *into* something that already exists). While the Panthers, still operating within a causalist Marxist framework that prioritized substructure over superstructure, viewed cultural nationalism as delaying the work of revolution, and Karenga himself insisted that Kawaida was *preparing* the way for revolution, in reality the Panthers and US were drawing

---

8   Federal Bureau of Investigation, United States Department of Justice, *US* (April 1968), 13, https://www.governmentattic.org/docs/FBI_Monograph_US_April-1968.pdf.

on and contributing to the radical imaginary in tandem. But to recognize this required another temporal construct, the time of radical alterity that unfolds in the creation of new forms, rather than revolutionary time, with its clearly defined before and after.

Interestingly, on the ground, Karenga pursued a politics of "operational unity" or "unity without uniformity" in respect to Black Power that in many ways resembled Newton's intercommunalism. Scot Brown argues that it also mirrored the "Basic Unity Program" Malcolm X outlined in his "Ballot or Bullet" speech, which didn't demand that organizations "become subordinate to or merge with one particular group, but rather accept the broad principles of black nationalism and simultaneously remain independent and autonomous."[9] Brown describes a 1967 Uhuru Day[10] rally in Watts where Karenga, H. Rap Brown (SNCC chair at the time), and Huey Newton all shared the same stage, each espousing the right to self-defense, self-respect, and self-determination in their own terms.[11] US also supported local autonomous actions, such as the ill-fated 1967 Freedom City campaign initiated by SNCC, with the goal of transforming Watts and surrounding neighborhoods into an independent Black-majority municipality.

Numerous Black Arts Movement writers and artists were influenced by Karenga in their creation of a revolutionary counterculture that drew simultaneously on precolonial African culture and the jazz avant-garde, while others mined the long tradition of African American popular culture, particularly blues and R&B music. And as Smethurst points out, some of the people most influenced by Karenga, notably Amiri Baraka, were also among the strongest proponents of Black popular culture. Indeed, Black Arts was a major force, argue Bracey Jr., Sanchez, and Smethurst, "in introducing the idea that 'high' art can be

---

9   Scot Brown, "The US Organization, Black Power Vanguard Politics, and the United Front Ideal: Los Angeles and Beyond," *Black Scholar* 31, nos. 3/4 (Fall/Winter 2001): 23.
10 Uhuru (Freedom) Day, another holiday created by US, commemorated the assassination of Malcolm X.
11 Brown, "US Organization, Black Power Vanguard Politics," 24.

popular in form and content and popular culture can be socially and artistically serious." [12]

Another prominent feature of BAM artistic production was the blurring of the boundaries between media and genres, which Smethurst analyzes with reference to the *Wall of Respect* mural created in 1967 by the Organization of Black American Culture Visual Arts workshop in Chicago. He describes the mural's striking blend of image and text, which centers Baraka's poem "SOS": "Did the mural remind viewers of the visuality of written poetry? Did the poem bring orality into what is not usually thought of as a sonic medium?"[13] The creation of the mural was a public performance that brought still more art forms together: "As the artists worked on the various sections of the mural, there were often performances of poetry, theater, music, and/or dance as the residents of Chicago's South Side watched and sometimes joined in to one degree or another."[20] At the mural's dedication, which included dance, music, poetry and political speeches, police sharpshooters looked down on the proceedings from the rooftops of nearby buildings, rendering Baraka's SOS, and the need to create spaces where it could be answered, all the more urgent:

> Calling black people
> Calling all black people, man woman child
> Wherever you are, calling you, urgent, come in
> Black People, come in, wherever you are, urgent, calling
> You, calling all black people
> Calling all black people, come in, black people, come
> On in.[14]

---

12 Bracey Jr., Sanchez, and Smethurst, "Editors' Introduction," 4.
13 James Smethurst, "Black Arts Movement," in *Keywords for African American Studies,* eds. Erica R. Edwards, Roderick A. Ferguson, and Jeffrey O.G. Ogbar (New York: NYU Press, 2018), 20.
14 Amiri Baraka, *Black Magic: Sabotage, Target Study, Black Art: Collected Poetry 1961–1967* (Indianapolis: Bobbs-Merrill, 1969), 115.

The mural form's public, spatial properties, its positioning outside the art market, and its capacity to reach a broad audience, made it a favorite of BAM visual artists. Bracey Jr., Sanchez, and Smethurst also flag poetry and theater as other art forms prominent within the movement, in part because of the ease with which they moved from one location to another. Whether printed in Black-run journals, newspapers, broadsides, and chapbooks, or performed at rallies, on street corners, and in community rooms, they generated solidarity and carved out a space for self-determination, inviting their audience to both "come in" and "come on in."

Black Arts literature in particular was highly experimental in its forms. As Carolyn Gerald describes, the point was "to experiment with different rhythms, with different syntactical forms, with a different vocabulary."[15] The freer the art — to defy literary convention, to play with typography, to draw on vernacular speech, to mix high art and popular culture, to intermingle with the other arts — the freer the people producing and receiving that art. One sees this ethos at work in Sonia Sanchez's "a/coltrane/poem":

> my favorite things
>   is u/blowen
>   yo/favorite/things
> stretchen the mind
>   till it bursts past the con/fines of
> solo/en melodies.[16]

For Fred Moten, the embrace of formal experimentation was and remains key to Black liberation, and is grounded in the Black experience, beginning with slavery:

---

[15] Carolyn Gerald, "Symposium: The Measure and the Meaning of the Sixties," in *SOS–Calling All Black People,* eds. Bracey Jr., Sanchez, and Smethurst, 46.

[16] Sonia Sanchez, *We a BaddDDD People* (Detroit: Broadside Press, 1973), 69.

> I feel like the figures that I would want to embrace and celebrate as these fundamental figures in the black radical and aesthetic tradition, they're all experimental, and part of it is because black social life is experimental — not only because of what it is that we have to make up, because of what it is we have to produce, what it is we have to survive within the context of a brutal anti-sociality or sociopathy which is invested in our death and in our living [...] [but because] our experimentation happens in and against the backdrop of our having been subjected to an experiment. You take 45, 50, 60, 70 however many million people and take them from one continent to another, that's a fucking experiment, you know? Some absolute mad scientist type of shit.[17]

There were authoritarian currents in BAM, particularly among those influenced by Karenga, who sought to determine where these experiments should go by imposing content restrictions on the art being made as well as authenticity requirements on the artists themselves. Musing in 1967 on the brief but important life of Baraka's Black Arts Theater, Harold Cruse suggests the project was undermined by a lack of respect for the "autonomy of art and art criticism, not as a static or universal value, but within the context of black power" — that is to say, as an integral part of the process of political autonomization. The "precise cultural aim" of the Black Power movement, Cruse maintained, "has to be for the enhancement of criticism and creativity, not the other way around."[18]

While BAM included many important women artists and writers, and embraced egalitarianism early on, in its later years Karenga's followers subscribed to a patriarchal vision of gender relations (supposedly) rooted in traditional African culture which suppressed women's participation. This led to conflict

---

[17] "An Interview with Fred Moten, Pt. II," *Literary Hub,* August 6, 2015, https://lithub.com/an-interview-with-fred-moten-pt-ii/.

[18] Harold Cruse, "The Harlem Black Arts Theater — New Dialogue with the Lost Black Generation," in *SOS–Calling All Black People,* eds. Bracey Jr., Sanchez, and Smethurst, 45.

within BAM and the birth of a new autonomism, Black Power/ Black Arts feminism, marked by the publication of Toni Cade Bambara's 1970 anthology *The Black Woman* and her landmark essay "On the Issue of Roles." "We profess to be about liberation," she observes, "but behave in a constricting manner; we rap about being correct but ignore the danger of having one half of our population regard the other with such condescension."[19] Bambara encouraged the movement to go further into autonomy, to get more creative: "Perhaps we need to face the terrifying and overwhelming possibility that there are no models, that we shall have to create from scratch" (though she suggests that another reading of the gender roles in the African societies Karenga draws upon is also possible).[20]

It would seem then that the work, and play, of autonomizing is never done — counter to James's argument that unity and revolution must wait until after all groups have made their autonomous power felt — for it is what continually expands the radical horizon. With Black Power and the Black Arts movement, the "different rhythms" of autonomization — political, cultural, and artistic — converged in a way that allowed many things to move, all at once and for a number of years. This was not *preparation* for revolution, but the making and doing of it. Baraka gets at this in his poem "It's Nation Time," which he always performed as a kind of voiced solo with other instruments, deploying the "changing same" of jazz improvisation. "Time to get / together / time to be one strong fast black energy space," he chants, evoking the time of poiēsis, that other time that music makes, that poetry makes, that politics makes, the time of individual-and-collective autonomy, radical creation time.[21]

---

19 Toni Cade Bambara, "On the Issue of Roles," in *The Black Woman: An Anthology*, ed. Toni Cade Bambara (Ann Arbor: University of Michigan Press, 1970), 103.
20 Ibid., 109.
21 For an in-depth analysis of Baraka's performances of "It's Nation Time," see Meta DuEwa Jones, "Politics, Process and (Jazz) Performance: Amiri Baraka's 'It's Nation Time,'" *African American Review* 37, nos. 2/3 (Summer-Autumn, 2003): 245–52.

EIGHTH LETTER

On the Fourth of July in Los Angeles

Dear A,

Last night was a good one, and by good one, I mean non-stop action, arrows shooting into the sky from the triangle in front of La Esquina, short stacks popping on the corner, fronds of light cascading over the ridge like multicolored palm trees. Wish you were here, though depending on your tolerance for loud noises, you may not feel the same.

On the Eastside of Los Angeles, which is where I live now, something fantastical happens on the Fourth of July. Beginning at sundown and continuing far into the night, fireworks — real fireworks, not firecrackers — erupt on every block. I've heard this all-over display described as *anarchic,* by which is meant signifying without logic, but I've always thought of it as *autonomous,* proceeding according to its own laws. Smoke fills the canyons and still they come, blue-green-red-and-yellow sparks showering the hillsides, a panoply of professional-grade pyrotechnics bearing little resemblance to the earthbound sparklers that count as homegrown entertainment in other parts of the country. The patterns in the night sky are both visual and sonic (proud whistles and booms, not sneaky rat-a-tat-tats), and they have a logic — no, they *have* a thousand logics. The speed with which they come, the shapes they make, the solos, the riffs, the awe-inspiring potlatches, finales that are final only for that block, for that house, for that person even, though friends and family usually pool their money to get more bang for their buck — could this be the look and sound of individual-and-collective autonomy?

When and where I grew up, fireworks were largely confined to stadiums and harbors, with only one or two displays in any given locale. They were stolidly municipal affairs, often sponsored by civic organizations. You *went to see* the fireworks, you didn't walk outside and find yourself surrounded by them. The authorities put on a nice, safe, contained display, with fire trucks at hand, and usually there was martial musical accompaniment, to stir our gratitude for the bomb, the firework's utilitarian counterpart, and the soldiers who "keep us free."

Here, there's also the echo of bombs in the bombas, but the feel of the thing is insurrectionary, not imperialist. It stands to reason that the most incendiary displays often take place in East LA, home to the largest working-class Chicanx/Mexicanx community in the U.S., which tried unsuccessfully to become its own city in 1960 and was for generations deprived of political representation, and where explosions of another order erupted in the late sixties with the Blowouts and the Moratorium. But it's possible to trace the insurrectionary origins of LA's fireworks displays even further and farther back to Mexico, where fireworks first arrived with the conquistadors but only became popular after Independence, first as a way of marking the anniversary of liberation, and then for every and any celebration. Today, over fifty thousand families in Mexico manufacture handmade, mostly illegal fireworks in artisanal workshops, largely concentrated in the town of Tultapec. Though Tultapec makes the news every few years for a devastating accident in the workshops or markets, Jose Guadalupe Solano Sanchez, a musician whose mother, father, and grandparents all work in pyrotechnics there, describes it as "a magical, marvelous town." "There are a lot of people who criticize this art," he admits, "but we see it differently. It's our daily life."[1]

---

[1] Samantha Schmidt, "Fireworks Tragedy: The 'Magical' Mexican Town Where Pyrotechnics Are Life — and Too Often Death," *Houston Chronicle*,

Why is it so hard to police pyrotechnics, whether in Mexico or the U.S.? Or to put it another way, what is it about fireworks that escapes the law? It's not merely a matter of spontaneity: there's planning and craft involved in their fabrication and display that could be curtailed or disrupted at any stage. Could it be that authorities prefer pretend bombs lobbed by marginalized and displaced people to real ones — the "gives-them-an-outlet" approach? But there are plenty of quieter "outlets": booze, shopping, screens. How do fireworks fly under the radar when they're lighting up the sky?

Perhaps they don't so much evade the radar as jam it. People must consent to be governed, and in this one thing, they don't consent. As Castoriadis famously observed, "If people didn't effectively adhere to the system, everything would collapse in the next six hours."[2] Even when the laws are "for their own safety," still, when it comes to fireworks, they don't consent. And then there's the question of the firework's ambiguous status as art or real life, "work" or "fire," which scrambles the signals, disrupts the hum of empire. It may be just for one night, but the sprawling show stymies the cops — and the citizen-cops who call 911 to complain — every time. How do you catch the "perps," when they're everywhere and nowhere? No, on this night, control of the city belongs to somebody (or somebodies) else. Sit back and enjoy the show.

We mustn't forget the dogs, though, who really suffer from the noise, cowering under couches and beds, clawing their way out of locked rooms, nor the occasional fires on the hillsides. As Castoriadis reminds us, any true instantiation of autonomy must be ecological, which is to say it must acknowledge "the basic fact that social life cannot fail to take into account in a pivotal way the environment in which social life unfolds."[3] The capital-

---

December 21, 2016, www.chron.com/news/nation-world/world/article/Fireworks-tragedy-The-magical-Mexican-town-10811226.php.

2 Cornelius Castoriadis, "From Ecology to Autonomy," in *The Castoriadis Reader*, ed. and trans. David Ames Curtis (Oxford: Blackwell, 1997), 241.

3 Cornelius Castoriadis, "The Revolutionary Force of Ecology," in *The Rising Tide of Insignificancy (The Big Sleep)*, trans. and ed. anonymously as a

ist project of total mastery over nature can only be countered by recognizing "the necessity of the self-limitation of [human beings] in relation to the planet upon which, by chance, [they exist], and which [they are] in the process of destroying."[4]

Indeed, nothing brings us closer to the abyss of meaninglessness, than the pre-social or "natural" world. Nature — however Anthropocene — "is always there as an inexhaustible provider of alterity and the always imminent risk of laceration of the web of significations with which society has lined it. The a-meaning of the world is always a possible threat for the meaning of society."[5] But it also provides the opportunity to recalibrate our practices and institutions from the ground up: Just think of how we behave in the wake of natural disasters — our suddenly unconditioned distribution of free food, water, and clothing, the suspension of our usual patterns of production and consumption.

Attention to the natural world and how we affect it, the dogs under the bed, the fires on the hillsides, helps us rethink our technologies and the uses we put them to — both the bomb and the bomba. It also underscores the need for a profound questioning of unlimited expansion as one of our society's core values, and a radically democratic reorientation toward self-limitation on both the individual and collective level.[6] As Castoriadis says, self-limitation is how we self-organize to keep from sawing off the branch on which we're sitting.[7]

The Fourth of July on the Eastside of Los Angeles thus ushers in a night of contradictions — including that of celebrating an "Independence Day" that resulted from and in the oppression of so many. But it also gives us a glimpse of autonomy, of how

---

      public service (n.p.: Not Bored, [2003]), 109, http://www.notbored.org/RTI.pdf.

4 Ibid., 121.

5 Cornelius Castoriadis, "Power, Politics, Autonomy," in *Philosophy, Politics, Autonomy: Essays in Political Philosophy*, ed. David Ames Curtis (New York: Oxford University Press, 1991), 152.

6 Castoriadis, "Revolutionary Force of Ecology," 116.

7 Ibid., 123.

deeply it can take root in a matter of hours, and how it might go deeper still. We must keep an eye (and ear) out for fugitive aesthetics like these, to share Harney and Moten's term, which escape carceral logic, creating the conditions "for a minute, for a day, of being able to hear something or see something or be with people in a way that right now we can't."[8] What would it mean for a shared creative practice or set of creative practices, including sociohistorical ones, to be, as in Tultapec, our daily life? I ask this question the morning of every fifth of July, still a bit incredulous that the night before actually happened, floating in the smoky space between what is and what, however briefly, just was.

---

[8] Made in China Journal, "Stefano Harney, Fred Moten, and Michael Sawyer: 'On Fugitive Aesthetics,'" *YouTube,* March 15, 2021, https://youtu.be/iBJh-9caNf4.

NINTH LETTER

Dear Teddy, Dear Herbert: On the Autonomy of Theory and of the University

Dear A,

I know this is not a correspondence, these kinds of letters never are, but I'm still thinking of you, writing to you, with urgency — urgency being the phase just prior to, and animated by, emergency. The phase where we can still think and write about what's happening, but in which demands are great that these thoughts and writings open out onto possibilities for action. To help shed some light on our situation, I'm going to center this letter on another set of letters, a true correspondence, between Theodor Adorno and Herbert Marcuse — or "Teddy" and "Herbert," as they addressed one another — at a moment when the autonomy of critical theory, and of the university itself, was under intense pressure.

Throughout spring and summer of 1969, the two friends and Frankfurt School colleagues were communicating about a series of disruptions to Adorno's lectures and the workings of the Institute for Social Research by members of the APO, or extraparliamentary opposition, a newly formed coalition of the German student and New Left movements which opposed the Vietnam War, supported Third World liberation movements, and sought to revolutionize Germany's conservative university and political cultures, which had never fully reckoned with the legacy of Nazism, while trying out new forms of political action and communal living. At the time of writing, Adorno was teaching at the Institute for Social Research and the University of Frankfurt, and Marcuse in the Philosophy Department at the University of California San Diego.

The first disruption to Adorno's class occurred at the beginning of the semester, when students occupied a room of the Institute and refused to leave. "It was dreadful," he bemoans in his letter to Marcuse. "We had to call the police, who then arrested all that they found in the room."[1] To his surprise, Marcuse condemns the Institute's response: "To put it brutally: if the alternative is the police or left-wing students, then I am with the students."[2] He reminds Adorno that "there are situations, moments, in which theory is pushed on further by praxis — situations and moments in which theory that is kept separate from praxis becomes untrue to itself," and insists that this one of them.[3] Though not a *revolutionary* situation, Marcuse concedes, the current state of society "is [still] so terrible, so suffocating and demeaning, that rebellion against it forces a biological, physiological reaction: one can bear it no longer, one is suffocating and one has to let some air in."

While agreeing that there can be moments in which theory is pushed on by practice, Adorno fires back at Marcuse that such a situation "neither exists objectively today, nor does the barren and brutal practicism that confronts us here have the slightest thing to do with theory anyhow." The one point he does take to heart is that a given situation could indeed be "so terrible one would have to attempt to break out of it, even if one recognizes the objective impossibility."[4] But neither is this that situation. As

---

[1] Theodor Adorno and Herbert Marcuse, "Correspondence on the German Student Movement," trans. Esther Leslie, *New Left Review* I/233 (January-February 1999): 124.

[2] Ibid., 125.

[3] Ibid.

[4] Ibid., 127.

a point of comparison, he observes: "We withstood in our time, you no less than me, a much more dreadful situation—that of the murder of the Jews, without proceeding to praxis, simply because it was blocked for us."

As the letters continue on, their disagreement moves onto the affective plane, with Adorno accusing Marcuse of deceiving himself as to how bad he thinks the situation really is. "I think that clarity about the streak of coldness in one's self is a matter for self-contemplation," he says. "To put it bluntly: I think that you are deluding yourself in being unable to go on without participating in the student stunts, because of what is occurring in Vietnam or Biafra."[5] Marcuse retorts, "in the light of the terrible situation I am unable to discover the 'cold streak in one's self.'"[6]

The figure of the "cold streak" that Adorno uses here to represent autonomy—specifically the "cold streak in oneself"—suggests that his notions of critical and (we shall see) artistic autonomy are paradoxically tied to a revolutionary horizon, on the one hand, and the bourgeois conception of personal autonomy, on the other, since the cold streak is essentially defined as being able to separate one's own fortunes from the fortunes of others. In *Negative Dialectics,* published just three years prior to this exchange, Adorno had revisited his famous statement that "after Auschwitz you could no longer write poems," saying that what he really meant to question was "whether after Auschwitz you can go on *living*—especially whether one who escaped by accident, one who by rights should have been killed, may go on living."[7] This is the context in which he first raises the specter of the cold streak: "His mere survival calls for the coldness, the basic principle of bourgeois subjectivity, without which there could have been no Auschwitz."[8]

It's clear that were Adorno to accept Marcuse's argument—that the current situation is so terrible that some action

---

5   Ibid.

6   Ibid., 129.

7   Theodor Adorno, *Negative Dialectics* (London: Taylor and Francis e-Library, 2004) 363.

8   Ibid.

must be taken against it and any action that is taken has at least some validity — he feels he would have to revisit his own response to the situation of the Holocaust, which was to move the Institute out of Nazi Germany (Marcuse in tow) and continue on with its work first in Switzerland and then the United States. But it's also clear that he perceives this route to survival — both individual and institutional — as politically and ethically compromised, a compromise that is justified only if the work of critical theory, which seeks to understand the social structures through which people are oppressed and exploited, continues along its autonomous track.

The next protest incident Adorno alludes to in his correspondence with Marcuse is the so-called "breast action" or *Busenaktion* (since there's a German word for every situation) in April, which his students conceived of as a moment of "planned tenderness" toward their professor. At the start of Adorno's lecture, a student walked up to the board and wrote: "He who only allows dear Adorno to rule will uphold capitalism his entire life," while three students wearing long leather jackets approached the podium, sprinkled rose and tulip petals over Adorno's head, and attempted to kiss him on the cheek while exposing their naked breasts to him.[9]

The *Busenaktion* was widely condemned, including by Adorno himself, as an attempt by the students to embarrass their professor, but we might alternatively consider it a calling forth of the "cold streak," a staging of the possibility Adorno himself raises: that rather than preserving the possibility of a utopian future in the midst of the awful present, the autonomy of theory — at least in that moment — was in fact acting in service of the preservation of bourgeois individualism and its awful past. And we should emphasize — though the few existing accounts do not — that this was an action undertaken by a group of women whose presence in Adorno's "Introduction to

---

9 "A Conversation with Theodor W. Adorno (Spiegel, 1969)," *Communists in Situ*, September 1, 2015, https://cominsitu.wordpress.com/2015/09/01/a-conversation-with-theodor-w-adorno-spiegel-1969/.

Dialectical Thinking" lectures was most likely unremarked up to that point, either in class or on the syllabus, which may have compounded the shock — and the effect — of it.

Still, Adorno can't see the student movement as anything other than near-sighted and haphazard. In a famous interview with *Der Spiegel* after suspending his lecture series due to these interruptions, he decries the notion that "if only you change little things here and there, then perhaps everything will be better."[10] But Marcuse, while conceding that the student movement is not a revolution, nonetheless affirms the need for their "new, very unorthodox forms of radical opposition."[11] Given that bourgeois democracy in Germany is sealed off from qualitative change through the parliamentary democratic process itself, he argues, "extra-parliamentary opposition becomes the only form of 'contestation'; 'civil disobedience,' direct action."[12] These forms of opposition no longer follow familiar patterns, but they must nonetheless be recognized as "letting the air in."[13]

It would seem, then, that Adorno's failures in this moment are both affective and aesthetic — he misrecognizes the tenderness of the *Busenaktion* as a "barren and brutal practicism," and he cannot see the radicality in the new forms of contestation. In response, Marcuse argues that what in fact the students are calling for is not practice *in lieu* of theory but a different formulation of the relationship between the two. "It is wrong to cling onto the difference [between theory and practice] in its previous form," he tells Adorno, "when this has changed in a reality that embraces (or opens up to) theory and practice."[14] To insist upon the old autonomy in this context, he suggests, is to deny "the internal political content, the internal political dynamic"[15] of the old theory, which is why students have come to them in search of concrete political positions to begin with.

---

10 Ibid.
11 Adorno and Marcuse, "Correspondence," 129.
12 Ibid., 130.
13 Ibid., 125.
14 Ibid., 129.
15 Ibid.

The debate they're having is a time-honored one: Is this a revolution or is this just activism? If it's revolution, we'll leave the lecture hall for the streets right now, but if not, we'll bide our time, continuing to exercise freedom of thought and expression in the classroom and making our contribution to liberation that way. But when (and how) does activism with revolutionary aims (as opposed to reformist ones) *become* revolution? And even if it never does, (Marcuse, for one, perceived Germany as incapable of the kind of revolutionary activity achieved in France), isn't it nonetheless making and doing something other than business as usual — something that can result in new autonomies? To ask that critical theory engage in this making and doing, as students did of Adorno, and to ask louder when refused, can be seen as a misguided militancy, but it can also be seen as the urgent calling forth of a new mode of instituting and a new mode of relating to society and the institution, in which professors and students find other ways of being (and not being) professors and students, further autonomizing the university as a force for radical social change.

Though more sympathetic to Adorno's position in his public addresses than in their private letters, in a May 1968 lecture at UCSD discussing recent events in Paris and Berlin, Marcuse professed himself "highly hesitant and highly reluctant to indict even the disagreeable and even the all-too prematurely radical features of the movement."[16] Unlike Adorno, he understood the student movement as attempting to "bridge the gap between a medieval, outdated mode of teaching and curriculum, and to meet the reality — the terrible and miserable reality — which is outside the classroom."[17] What's more, he perceived it as a "total protest," though sparked by specific issues, "a protest against the entire system of values, against the entire system of objectives, against the entire system of performances required and prac-

---

16 Herbert Marcuse, "Herbert Marcuse and the Student Revolts of 1968: An Unpublished Lecture," *Jacobin,* March 2021, https://jacobinmag.com/2021/03/herbert-marcuse-student-revolts-of-1968-ucsd-lecture.

17 Ibid.

ticed in established society. [...] [I]t is a refusal to accept — to continue to accept [....] [n]ot only the economic conditions, not only the political institutions, but the entire system of values which they feel is rotten at the core."[18]

Marcuse makes note of the fact that the events of May '68 were touched off by police invading the campus of the Sorbonne to quell student protests for the first time in the university's history. Today, the autonomous university as it continues to exist (at least as a concept) in Europe, Mexico, and other countries may seem entirely out of reach in a U.S. context where universities are so fully penetrated by police as to house their own police forces. But perhaps for this very reason, the questions Adorno and Marcuse urgently debated in their letters as to the revolutionary potential of that autonomy are ever more relevant today.

---

18 Ibid.

TENTH LETTER

On Art's Autonomy, Frankfurt School-Style

Dear A,

Not at all coincidentally, during the period of their correspondence on the autonomy of theory and of the university, Adorno and Marcuse were also reflecting intently on the autonomy of *art*—Adorno in his final book, *Aesthetic Theory*, published posthumously in 1970; Marcuse in his 1969 *Essay on Liberation*. Though these reflections took the form of monographs and not letters, they continued the conversation where it left off, moving on from considering the role of critical theory in revolutionary struggle to considering the role of art.

For Adorno, "Art must be and wants to be utopia, and the more utopia is blocked by the real functional order, the more this is true."[1] As Jackson Petsche notes, he is invested in the radical break with existing society that aestheticism brought about, with "art for art's sake" as its mantra, even as he tries to turn that break to political purpose.[2] But in order to serve a political func-

---

1 Theodor Adorno, *Aesthetic Theory*, trans. Robert Hullot-Kentor (Minneapolis: University of Minnesota Press, 1996), 41.
2 Jackson Petsche, "The Importance of Being Autonomous: Toward a Marxist Defense of Art for Art's Sake," *Mediations: Journal of the Marxist Literary Group* 26, nos. 1–2 (Fall–Spring 2013): 143–58.

tion, art's utopia, embodied in its forms, must always be out of sync with society — only in this way does it retain its element of imagined freedom: "If the utopia of art were fulfilled," Adorno maintains, "it would be art's temporal end."[3] The more formally innovative, or "avant-garde" the art, the more it challenges the existing society and prepares the way for a better one.

Marcuse understands the function of art vis-à-vis society in similar terms, as a utopian "great refusal" of all that is: "The work of art [...] re-presents reality while accusing it."[4] But in *Essay on Liberation*, he takes a different tack when it comes to the relationship between art and politics, hailing the emergence of a "New Sensibility" in society that matches the intensity of the aesthetic Great Refusal with a political Great Refusal, a break with the established order that he sees as foundational to the spread of liberation movements around the globe. He describes this break elsewhere with reference to Maurice Blanchot's 1958 essay "Refusal," published during the Algerian crisis, in which Blanchot declares: "There is a reason which we no longer accept, there is an appearance of wisdom which horrifies us, there is a plea for agreement and conciliation which we will no longer heed. A break has occurred. We have been reduced to that frankness which no longer tolerates complicity."[5]

Fast-forwarding to 1969, Marcuse raises the possibility that "political protest, having assumed a total character, [now] reaches into a dimension which, as aesthetic dimension, has been essentially apolitical."[6] Unlike Adorno, then, he entertains the notion that art — at least in this moment and situation — is actually in a position to shape social reality. With the birth of the New Sensibility, which we can equate more or less to the counterculture, "the radical social content of the aesthetic needs

---

3 Adorno, *Aesthetic Theory*, 41.
4 Herbert Marcuse, *The Aesthetic Dimension: Toward a Critique of Marxist Aesthetics* (Boston: Beacon, 1977), 8.
5 Herbert Marcuse, *One-Dimensional Man: Studies in the Ideology of Advanced Industrial Society* (1964; repr., Boston: Beacon, 2012), 256.
6 Herbert Marcuse, *Essay on Liberation* (Boston: Beacon, 1969), 30.

becomes evident as the demand for their most elementary satisfaction is translated into group action on an enlarged scale."[7]

If there's one artistic practice of the late sixties and early seventies that might be said to embody Marcuse's New Sensibility, it's that of so-called "living art," in particular the art of the Living Theatre, which sought to free the energy of the theater from its moribund conventions by jettisoning authorship and the dramatic script, and involving the audience in the performance event — transforming the theater, as Bradford Martin observes, from a site of enactment into a site of action.[8] In 1968, while in residence in Sicily, the Living Theatre created the most ambitious and controversial embodiment of their ideas, a production whose title, *Paradise Now,* might be said to troll Adorno avant la lettre. Largely unscripted, *Paradise Now* consisted of eight "performance situations," each of which included a rite and a vision performed by Living Theatre actors and an action performed by the audience with the support of the actors. In addition to inviting audience members to participate in naked "body piles" as part of the rung of "Universal Intercourse," the production ended by throwing open the doors of the theater and leading a procession of naked and half-naked people outside, chanting "The theatre is in the street. The street belongs to the people. Free the theatre. Free the street. Begin,"[9] frequently resulting in arrests for indecent exposure.

But in point of fact, Marcuse and Adorno were united in their disdain for the living art — or art as life — movement, and especially the Living Theatre. Adorno raised the specter of fascism: "It is claimed that the age of art is over: now it is a matter of realizing its truth content, which is facilely equated with art's

---

7 Ibid., 27–28.
8 See Bradford Martin's discussion of "collective creation" in "Politics as Art, Art as Politics: The Freedom Singers, the Living Theatre and Public Performance," in *Long Time Gone: Sixties America Then and Now,* ed. Alexander Bloom (Oxford: Oxford University Press, 2001), 159–88.
9 Bradford Martin, *The Theater Is in the Street: Politics and Public Performance in 1960s America* (Amherst: University of Massachusetts Press, 2004), 49.

social content: The verdict is totalitarian."[10] Marcuse was more sympathetic to its aims, which he recognized as reflecting the New Sensibility: "The distance and dissociation of art from reality are denied, refused, and destroyed; if art is still anything at all, it must be real, part and parcel of life — but of a life which is itself the conscious negation of the established way of life."[11]

Though willing, at least for a time, to envision a different relationship between theory and practice, Marcuse was quite convinced that what he perceived as a rebellion against the autonomy of art, while understandable, "only succeed[ed] in a loss of artistic quality; illusory destruction, illusory overcoming of alienation."[12] He found the audience participation encouraged by the Living Theatre, for instance, to be "spurious and the result of previous arrangements," and the vaunted transformation of the audience's consciousness and behavior to be merely part of the play. Most of all, he faulted living art for the naive belief that it could erase the boundary between art and reality, since "it must retain, no matter how minimally, the Form of Art as different from non-art." The true avant-garde, he argued, is not "those who try desperately to produce the absence of Form and the union with real life, but rather those who do not recoil from the exigencies of Form, who find the new word, image, and sound which are capable of 'comprehending' reality as only Art can comprehend and negate it."[13]

To a large extent, Marcuse, like Adorno, identifies avant-gardism with the oeuvres of individual artists — Beckett, Schoenberg, Picasso among them — and defends the realm of subjectivity, of "inwardness, emotions and the imagination," against the charge that subjectivity is itself a bourgeois notion. "With the affirmation of the inwardness of subjectivity," he argues, "the individual steps out of the network of exchange relationships

---

10 Adorno, *Aesthetic Theory*, 251.
11 Herbert Marcuse, "Art as Form of Reality," in *Art and Liberation*, Collected Papers of Marcuse 4 (London: Routledge, 2006), 141.
12 Ibid., 146.
13 Ibid.

and exchange values, withdraws from the reality of bourgeois society, and enters another dimension of existence."[14] He is careful to say, however, that "withdrawal and retreat [are] not the last position," noting that even in bourgeois society, subjectivity has striven to "break out of its inwardness into the material and intellectual culture."[15] Indeed, under totalitarianism, it becomes a political value, a "counterforce against aggressive and exploitative socialization." [16]

What Marcuse aims to counter is a reductive tendency he perceives in Marxist thought to dissolve the subjectivity of individuals — "their own consciousness and unconscious" — into class consciousness, which minimizes a major prerequisite of revolution: "namely, the fact that the need for radical change must be rooted in the subjectivity of individuals themselves, in their intelligence and their passions, their drives and their goals."[17] But the autonomy he champions remains trapped within the opposition of the individual to mass society, rather than linking the individual and the collective in new and liberatory ways, also a prerequisite for revolution. It's true that under totalitarianism, when all praxis is blocked, as Adorno describes, the "other dimension of existence" constituted by subjectivity can have a political effect. It does so, however, not merely by rendering the *individual* visible once more but also by reviving the possibility of *forms of collectivity* that allow for the flourishing of individuals (samizdat provides one example of this).

As noted above, in the aesthetic register, Marcuse's notion of autonomy is firmly aligned with the individual artist; more precisely, with works of art that are recognizably the product of a single artist, and within that subset, works that demonstrate "aesthetic form," or the transformation of "a given content (actual or historical, personal or social fact) into a self-contained whole: a poem, play, novel, etc."[18] This world-unto-itself of the

---

14 Marcuse, *Aesthetic Dimension*, 4.
15 Ibid.
16 Ibid.
17 Ibid., 3.
18 Ibid., 8.

art work ensures that it is "taken out of the constant process of reality and assumes a significance and truth of its own."[19] Art's truth, he maintains, "lies in its power to break the monopoly of established reality to define what is real."[20]

But the process by which this break with established reality achieved by aesthetic rupture "translates" into revolutionary struggle is not addressed by either Marcuse or Adorno. Rather, they adhere to what Gabriel Rockhill calls the talisman complex, imbuing the single artwork with "a sovereign political power."[21] This approach, Rockhill notes, "largely dismisses the complex variability of social dynamics in favor of a more or less monocausal determination: each work of art produces a singular political effect."[22] In the case of Frankfurt School aesthetics, this effect would be opening people's eyes to the alienation, brutality, and unfreedom of capitalist society, while at the same time providing them with a modicum of freedom and fulfillment, as a sort of taster for the liberated society to come.[23]

In fact, Rockhill argues, the talisman complex is just as reductive as the vulgar Marxist paradigm Marcuse is trying to challenge, since it ignores the social apparatus surrounding works of art, which is so often the target of avant-garde practices. In addition to and often as an element *of* formal experimentation, avant-gardes have historically attempted to introduce novel modes of production, circulation, and reception, "reworking the social status of art and its position in a matrix of political, economic and technological relations."[24] Seen through this lens, Marcuse's insistence that living art is itself formless or *against* form — as opposed to invested in developing *new forms* that both challenge the institution of art and activate art's social dimension in a political way, its "social politicity," as Rockhill

---

19 Ibid.
20 Ibid., 9.
21 Gabriel Rockhill, *Radical History and the Politics of Art* (New York: Columbia University Press, 2014), 64.
22 Ibid.
23 Ibid.
24 Ibid., 133.

refers to it — reveals the limitations of his formal vocabulary, which does not or cannot account for any of these innovations.

Given their emphasis on the individual artist, the "complete" work of art, and their measuring of the revolutionary potential of art in terms of its distance from actual revolutionary politics, it actually stands to reason that both Adorno and Marcuse would loathe the innovations of the Living Theatre, which sought in its practices to challenge the auteur, the script, and the purging of all recognizable political content from art. In "Meditation on Acting and Anarchism," Living Theatre cofounder Julian Beck ponders the problem of the authoritarian position of the director, and describes the various ways the company tried to achieve a process whereby "the performers directed themselves thru the medium of the director."[25] One such strategy was "collective creation," or devising/writing the play as a group, the process they used to generate *Paradise Now,* others were open-ended audience participation and improvisational performance.

Street Songs, a piece included in *Mysteries and Smaller Pieces,* and derived from a score by Fluxus poet Jackson MacLow, asks the performer to recite march slogans of the day in a kind of call and response with the audience. There's a characteristic looseness of form to the piece as performed by the Living Theatre, and at first glance, obvious political content — chants of "Freedom Now" "Stop the War," "A bas la guerre," etc. — but what is performed is in fact the inverse movement of *Paradise Now,* where art is turned out of the theater into the street. Rather, through this brief ritual, the street is brought into the theater, and marching chants become the meditation mantras of a single cross-legged performer, Julian Beck.

All sorts of questions present themselves: Do the chants gain or lose meaning when funneled through a single voice? Is the company/audience mocking or supporting Beck in his utopian aspirations? Is he himself endorsing or satirizing the political sentiments he vocalizes? Is he embracing or critiquing the form

---

25 Julian Beck, *The Life of the Theatre* (Ann Arbor: University of Michigan Press, 2008), 48.

of the chant itself? Is he communing with fellow revolutionaries or confronting the audience with its own passivity? The meaning of the piece isn't overdetermined or overscripted by its politics in the way Marcuse describes, for even as it brings street chants into the theater, it changes their form, opening it up to questioning and, potentially, transformation. *Street Songs* consciously exploits the *difference* between art and life (songs and chants), while at the same time rendering that border more porous. It calls attention to the social processes of production, circulation, and reception of art that Rockhill makes visible, democratizing them without relinquishing their difference, opening aesthetic autonomy out onto political autonomy.[26]

There is a whole world—or array of worlds—here that the talisman complex erases,[27] a set of processes and practices into which intervention is also required if the formal experimentation Marcuse and Adorno champion is actually to play a part in the creation of new institutions and new modes of instituting that revolutionary struggle requires. As Rockhill notes, the bracketing of the social relations at work in aesthetic and political practices continues to be one of the core problems of debates on art and politics today, and one which "casts a long shadow over the social complex in which diverse dimensions of aesthetic and political practices overlap, entwine, and sometimes merge."[28] It is these worlds the autonomy project seeks to uncover.

---

26 The Living Theatre was known for its experiments in communal living and longstanding engagement with anarcho-pacifism.

27 Some of which are famously depicted in Howard Becker's ethnography *Art Worlds* (Berkeley: University of California Press, 1982).

28 Rockhill, *Radical History and the Politics of Art*, 6.

ELEVENTH LETTER

On Being Apart Together and Being Together Apart

Dear A,

From here on out, as these letters move closer to the present, I think you may find they're a bit all-over-the-place-and-all-at-once, but there's a reason for this. Praxis, as Castoriadis reminds us, seeks out "the grooves, lines of force, veins, which mark out the possible, the feasible, indicate the probable, and permit action to find points of support in the given."[1] It's the tracing of making and doing, yes, through history, but also across the social landscape at a particular moment in time. And of course, it has its idiosyncrasies. Perhaps after all this is merely my personal psychogeography of the Now — but isn't that another way of saying "letter"?

Let's start by revisiting one recent battle over the autonomy of art, critically speaking, which occurred in response to the explosion of socially engaged art in the late nineties and early oughts that was explicitly "relational" in its orientation. These battles

---

1 Cornelius Castoriadis, "Marxism and Revolutionary Theory," in *The Castoriadis Reader,* ed. and trans. David Ames Curtis (Oxford: Blackwell, 1997), 154.

are always a sign that something is happening, or about to happen, in society at large, and are well worth returning to.

Curator Nato Thompson describes this "social turn" in art via a trajectory beginning with *relational aesthetics* — short-lived participatory events in museum and gallery contexts — and extending through to *social practice* — local, community-based, and more long-term social interventions. In general, this current in art was "deeply intertwined in participation, sociality, conversation, and 'the civic.'"[2] Thompson himself was an important curator of these kinds of practices, particularly the more "interventionist" ones, and organized two important exhibitions/conferences at Creative Time, *Democracy in America* (2008) and *Living as Form* (2011), that helped to clarify this tendency.[3]

Grant Kester, in essays and books such as *Conversation Pieces: Community and Communication in Modern Art* and *The One and The Many: Contemporary Collaborative Art in a Global Context,* formulates this development positively as a shift in emphasis, on the one hand, from the "artwork qua object" onto a dialogical aesthetics attuned to the "very process of communication that the artwork catalyzes"[4] and, on the other, from the authorial status of the artist onto collaborative creative practices among artists and between artists and audiences. These practices and aesthetics, he argues, challenged the "conventional, dyadic structure in which the avant-garde artist engenders consciousness in an unenlightened viewer," and experimented with new forms of collectivity and agency.[5] A project representative of the dialogical aesthetic would be Suzanne Lacy, Annice Jaco-

---

2   Ibid., 19.
3   Nato Thompson, "Living as Form," in *Living as Form: Socially Engaged Art From 1991–2011,* ed. Nato Thompson (New York: Creative Time, 2012), 31.
4   Grant Kester, *Conversation Pieces: Community and Communication in Modern Art* (Berkeley: University of California Press, 2004), 90.
5   Grant Kester, "The Sound of Breaking Glass, Part II: Agonism and the Taming of Dissent," *e-flux* 31 (January 2012), http://www.e-flux.com/journal/the-sound-of-breaking-glass-part-ii-agonism-and-the-taming-of-dissent/.

by, and Chris Johnson's *The Roof Is on Fire,* which brought together two hundred California high school students for a series of dialogues on the roof of an Oakland parking garage to discuss problems facing BIPOC young people.[6] Here, art provided the context for Oakland youth to discuss their experiences without a predetermined goal or outcome. An exemplar of experimental engagement with new forms of collectivity and agency would be Park Fiction, a long-term project spanning the late nineties and early oughts, which invited Hamburg residents and community organizations to join a "parallel planning process," imagining a park (and bringing it into being through subsequent actions) in a space where developers planned to put up high-rise apartments and office buildings.[7] In this situation, art provided the frame for new forms of self-organization that put pressure on a top-down, developer-dominated planning process.

In a series of essays and her book *Artificial Hells: Participatory Art and the Politics of Spectatorship* (2011), Claire Bishop evaluates the social turn rather less positively than Kester, as a move toward "participatory art" in which "the activation of the audience is positioned against its mythic counterpart, passive spectatorial consumption."[8] She decries a perceived tendency on the part of artists and curators to judge this work on the basis of its practical effects, be they the creation of viable models for ethical collaboration or actual changes in public policy. "Consensual collaboration is valued over artistic mastery and individualism, regardless of what the project sets out to do or actually achieves," she argues, and "art enters a realm of useful, ameliorative and ultimately modest gestures, rather than the creation of singular acts that leave behind them a troubling wake."[9] When it comes to relational art, Bishop herself valorizes ideologically

---

6 Kester, *Conversation Pieces,* 4.
7 Grant Kester, *One and The Many: Contemporary Collaborative Art in a Global Setting* (Durham: Duke University Press, 2011), 24.
8 Claire Bishop, "Participation as Spectacle: Where Are We Now?" in Thompson, *Living as Form,* 36.
9 Claire Bishop, *Artificial Hells: Participatory Art and the Politics of Spectatorship* (London: Verso, 2011), 23.

opaque work that foregrounds the role of the artist-director and engages in traditional avant-garde shock tactics. A paradigmatic example would be Christopher Schlingensief's *Please Love Austria* (2000), for which Schlingensief erected a shipping container outside of the Vienna Opera House to house a group of asylum seekers whose activities were then web-televised, generating a public outcry from both sides of the political spectrum.[10]

Bishop argues that the kinds of social practices Kester advocates, while seeking to counteract the hyperindividualism of neoliberal capitalism, were easily integrated into the ideologically expansive but in actuality quite limited participatory frameworks of both liberal democracy and the knowledge/sharing economy. In Europe, they were happily absorbed into neoliberal government programs of the mid-2000s; in the U.S., by museum education departments reorienting toward an interactive/entertainment model of public interface. She contends that participatory or relational art lacks "both a social and an artistic target; in other words, participatory art today stands without a relation to an existing political project (only to a loosely defined anti-capitalism) and presents itself as oppositional to visual art by trying to side-step the question of visuality."[11] Rather than artists bearing the burden of "devising new models of social and political organization," she suggests, "the task today is to produce a viable international alignment of leftist political movements *and* a reassertion of art's inventive forms of negation as valuable in their own right."[12]

Bishop's arguments are useful insofar as they indicate the need for a different way of critically evaluating the social turn, other than in terms of its perceived effects on civic processes or social dynamics, which results from or leads to a politics of amelioration (on the part of both the artists and their critics). These art works or practices should be evaluated in formal terms, but the forms they take require a different vocabulary

---

10 Ibid., 279.
11 Ibid., 284.
12 Ibid.

because they are actually interventions into the institution of art and art's social politicity, and this is the ground on which they stand or fall. To fall back on art's necessary "visuality" and the shopworn version of the avant-garde as the scourge of bourgeois sensibilities is to ignore the possibilities of these practices and, in doing so, to miss their meaning.

Bishop's critique is strongly influenced by the philosopher Jacques Rancière, who was also skeptical of the social turn in art. While Kester wryly suggests Rancière emerged as an art world favorite at this time because his work provides theoretical validation for an "already cherished set of beliefs about the 'political' function of the artwork,"[13] he did seem to offer up something that was needed at the time: a defense of the autonomy of art that wasn't pure formalism, at least on its face, but which allowed for art's difference from politics while at the same including it in the larger political project of "redistributing the sensible."

Rancière uses the term "distribution of the sensible" to describe "the system of self-evident facts of sense perception that simultaneously discloses the existence of something in common and the delimitations that define the respective parts and positions within it."[14] Art changes our relationships to this something-in-common by intervening in the general distribution of ways of doing and making.[15] Politics similarly contests the distribution of the sensible, revolving around "what is seen and what can be said about it, around who has the ability to see and the talent to speak, around the properties of spaces and the possibilities of time."[16] The political moment, for Rancière, is when those whose subjectivity is normally obscured by *police consensus* — the hierarchical distribution of the visible and the sayable — rise up and make themselves seen and heard, thereby

---

13 Ibid., 81.
14 Jacques Rancière, "The Distribution of the Sensible: Politics and Aesthetics," in *The Politics of Aesthetics: The Distribution of the Sensible,* ed. Gabriel Rockhill (London: Continuum 2004), 13.
15 Ibid.
16 Ibid.

creating *dissensus,* "the demonstration (manifestation) of a gap in the sensible itself." Both politics and art thus engage in a reconfiguration of the things we hold in common — the former reconfiguring which groups or subjectivities are endowed with speech and visibility, the latter reconfiguring the fabric of sensory experience on the level of the object and the individual.[17] And they both do so in the direction of equality — equality of aesthetic forms and subject matter, equality of intelligences, and equality among members of society.

Rancière's interventions into art discourse, beginning with the publication of *The Politics of Aesthetics* (2005), were widely seen as having brought back into view both the specificity of art *and* its connection to politics. "Art and politics are not two permanent and separate realities about which it might be asked if they must be put in relation to one another," he maintains. "They are two forms of distribution of the sensible."[18] Their relationship is made possible by what he calls the "aesthetic regime" of the arts in the modern era, wherein art is defined as a specific "sensorium" at the same time that it is continually merging with other forms of activity and being.

But while he insists that aesthetics and politics together define the sensible delimitation of what is held in common, Rancière endows only politics with the ability to affect and shape collectivities. Art, he argues, traffics in the "modes of *that* and *I,* from which emerge the proper worlds of political *wes.*"[19] Like Bishop, he views art's indifference to social outcome as both the source and the guarantee of its subversive effects, because this alone ensures it will remain free from the pressures of police

---

[17] Jacques Rancière, "The Paradoxes of Political Art," in *Dissensus: On Politics and Aesthetics,* ed. and trans. Steven Corcoran (London: Bloomsbury 2010) 140.

[18] Jacques Rancière, *Aesthetics and Its Discontents,* trans. Steven Corcoran (Cambridge: Polity, 2009), 25–26.

[19] Gabriel Rockhill, "Rancière's Productive Contradictions: From the Politics of Aesthetics to the Social Politicity of Artistic Practice," *Symposium* 15, no. 2 (Fall 2011): 36. The text cited is not included in the English translation of Rancière's Le spectateur emancipé, but appears on pp. 65–66 of the original.

consensus. But as Rockhill observes, while Rancière "appears to have opened the door to a radically new conceptualization of the relationship between aesthetics and politics," when he separates the aesthetic modes of *that* and *I* from political *wes,* "he leads us to a door that he has locked and bolted from the inside, leaving art and politics proper cut off from one another."[20]

Significantly, in order to "prove" that art on its own can never generate a "we," Rancière goes to war on theater, which he defines broadly as "any form of performance that places bodies in action in front of an assembled audience."[21] More specifically, he must refute theater's claims to be an exemplary community form. The association of theater with "living community" is in his eyes a dubious romantic notion that valorizes "a way of occupying a place and a time as the body in action as opposed to a mere apparatus of laws; a set of perceptions, gestures and attitudes that precede and pre-form laws and political institutions."[22] It is the theater's outsized association with the romantic idea of aesthetic revolution, "changing not the mechanics of the state and laws, but the sensible forms of human experience," that Rancière must undo if he is to restore art to its proper domain.

He does so by rethinking theater's audience as a collection of individuals, arguing that "in front of a performance, just as in a museum, school or street, there are only ever individuals plotting their own paths in the forest of things, acts and signs that confront or surround them. [...] This shared power of the equality of intelligence links individuals, makes them exchange their intellectual adventures, in so far as it keeps them separate from one another."[23] By emphasizing their fundamental separation while downplaying the collective setting of the work (and the collaborative aspect of the performance), he recasts the experience of the theater, not as one of "being together," but of "being apart together."

---

20 Rockhill, "Rancière's Productive Contradictions," 36.
21 Jacques Rancière, *The Emancipated Spectator,* trans. Gregory Elliot (London: Verso, 2011), 2.
22 Ibid., 6.
23 Ibid., 17.

When it comes to contemporary artistic practices that engage with forms of collectivity, Rancière's primary targets are "political art" that makes viewers aware of already articulated political positions and "relational art" that presumes ideal community can be fashioned and lived through artistic practices without political conflict. He insists that these notions of art's politics discard the "original disjunction" that in fact makes it art — its suspension of cause and effect. For Rancière, as for Bishop, (as for Adorno), the individual remains the sole site of this necessary undecidability, such that the only political work to which art may really lay claim is that of "dis-identification," the canceling out of any form of political subjectivation by new forms of individuation. Art's vaunted suspension of cause and effect is inexorably tied to the ontological separation of the individual and the collective. Art forms like the theater, which trouble this separation, must be neutralized by Rancière's analysis.

In a notable passage from the *Emancipated Spectator,* he describes his surprise at reading a correspondence between two workers from the 1830s and discovering that rather than supplying "information on working conditions and forms of class consciousness," the two workers instead discuss only their enjoyment of the landscape's "forms and light and shade" and their own philosophical musings as "strollers and contemplators."[24] For Rancière, the workers' attention to aesthetic over political matters is proof that "they disrupted the distribution of the sensible which would have it that those who work do not have time to let their steps and gazes roam at random; and that the members of a collective body do not have time to spend on the forms and insignia of individuality."[25]

But what of the fact that one of the workers is writing about his daily life in a Saint-Simonian utopian community and the other is describing how he enjoyed his time off from the factory with two companions? Their aesthetic experiences are taking place, and being described to one another, within a social

---

24 Ibid., 19.
25 Ibid.

context that in its autonomous dimension allows them to enjoy both *being apart together* and *being together apart*. As Rockhill argues, "one of the core problems in Rancière's project is that he largely — though not entirely — removes art from its social inscription in his analysis of its relationship to politics."[26]

Steve Corcoran, in his introduction to *Dissensus: On Politics and Aesthetics,* acknowledges the "chance-like" nature of Rancièrian politics, which he attributes to the fact that "*nothing* explains why people decide to rise up and demonstrate their equality with those who rule. Every political moment involves the incalculable leap of those who decide to demonstrate their equality and organize their refusal against the injustices that promote the status quo" (italics his).[27] But, of course, this is only true if we ignore the *ongoing* work of autonomy, of radical creativity on both the individual (psychic) level and the collective level, which provides the experiences of unfolding freedom and equality that are foreclosed by existing structures. Perhaps it's not a matter of an incalculable leap toward demonstrating equality but of that demonstration proceeding from what has already been demonstrated elsewhere.

In a 2017 interview in *Ballast,* Rancière states: "Democracy is nothing other, basically, than the recollection of the meaning of anarchism. […] I have a profoundly anarchist sensibility but I separate it from little anarchist groups." His anarchism, he goes on to say, is rooted in autonomy: "Anarchism is first autonomy. It is cooperatives of production and consumption, autonomous forms of transmission of knowledge and information in relation to the reigning dominant logic. It is independence with respect to the governmental sphere."[28] I have to think that this anarchist sensibility is what led Rancière to view art as a site of political possibility, but in insisting on a non-relation between the modes

---

26 Gabriel Rockhill, *Radical History and the Politics of Art* (New York: Columbia University Press, 2014), 181.

27 Ibid., 9.

28 The interview is posted online as Julius Gavroche, "Jacques Rancière: The Anarchy of Democracy," *Autonomies,* May 10, 2017, https://autonomies.org/2017/05/jacques-ranciere-the-anarchy-of-democracy/.

of "that and I" and that of "we," he centers the well-worn conflict of individual versus collective rather than the ongoing struggle between individual-and-collective autonomies (which could indeed be "little anarchist groups") and the heteronomies that suppress them. This blinds him — and his most astute readers, like Bishop — to the continual emergence of new forms of both politics and art that have the radical social imaginary as their shared horizon.

TWELFTH LETTER

On Art, Affect, and Occupy

Dear A,

Remember Occupy? How, for that brief period in late 2011, encampments appeared in every city and hamlet of the United States with the express intention of starting all over? Of course, it's easy, perhaps imperative within the capitalist imaginary, to forget moments like these when the sands shift, when the magma flows, when, as Marcuse says, the monopoly of established reality is broken, and when, as Marcuse also said, politics joins art in a great refusal of all that is.

The first time I walked into Occupy LA, in October of 2011, I remember feeling both at home and displaced: at home in the middle of this action that resembled so many of the art events I'd taken part in during the years prior, all of those shared meals and informal classes and giveaways of books and art and clothing; displaced because now that those practices had been absorbed into political activity, what was there for artists to do? The LA occupation hosted a free kitchen, a library, a medical tent, and a screen printing station, where my husband and I got our toddler's jean jacket stamped with a stenciled 99%. In this becoming-place/place of becoming, art was suddenly no longer a specialization but a generalized practice, and I had the feeling of having entered into Marcuse's "art as form of reality," the active fashioning of society according to aesthetic principles that takes place in the process of revolutionary struggle.

The imperative to transform the space, to *hold* it via that transformation, was palpable, as it had been and would be throughout the movement of the squares touched off by the 2008 economic crisis and the austerity measures and bailouts of banks and corporations that followed.¹ The DIY aesthetics of the encampment issued a similar exhortation, flagging it as a space of becoming whose meaning was open to determination by any and all. The invitation to speak, to "make your sign," was extended up front; the location of a sign-making area at the camp's perimeter framed the activities within. PEOPLE'S NEEDS BEFORE CORPORATE GREED / EVERY MORNING 99% WAKE UP ON THE WRONG SIDE OF CAPITALISM / THEY CONTROL YOUR FOOD-YOUR SCHOOLS-YOUR MEDICINE-YOUR MONEY-YOUR MEDIA-TAKE IT BACK. Most Occupy signs offered pointed criticism of the political system rather than demands for change within it — I CAN'T AFFORD MY OWN POLITICIAN SO I MADE THIS SIGN — signaling that what lay beyond was an act of political rather than civil disobedience, performing not resistance to particular elected officials, policies, laws and/or their unequal enforcement but, in Bernard Harcourt's words, a refusal "of the very way in which we are governed."²

The duration of the occupation — its durational *form* — was itself an act of political disobedience, going beyond other un-

---

1 Ayelen, a participant in Spain's 15M movement, describes the occupation of the Plaza del Sol as follows: "These were times that you'd go to the plaza on one day, and then when you returned on the next day seven hundred new things had come up. I remember one day I got there and I was told, 'They built a vegetable garden,' and I said, 'A vegetable garden?!' And yes, it was there, in the fountain of the Plaza del Sol of Madrid! And suddenly there was a nursery, and a library, and [...] it was fascinating. There was this thing about doing. Doing, doing and doing." Marina Sitrin and Dario Azzelini, *Occupying Language: The Secret Rendezvous with History and the Present* (Brooklyn: Zuccotti Park, 2012), 95.

2 Bernard E. Harcourt, "Political Disobedience," in W.J.T. Mitchell, Bernard E. Harcourt, and Michael Taussig, *Occupy: Three Inquiries in Disobedience* (Chicago: University of Chicago Press, 2013), 46.

permitted actions like the protest march and the sit-in to acquire its own spatial and temporal dimensions. For me, Occupy (LA) acquired a whole new level of meaning when I returned to the site and found it was *still there*. Contrasting the form of Occupy with its most immediate precursor, the event-oriented alter-globalization movement, Jodi Dean observes: "People have the opportunity to be more than spectators. After learning of an occupation, they can join. The event isn't over; it hasn't gone away. Implying a kind of permanence, occupation is ongoing. People are in it till 'this thing is done' — until the basic practices of society, of the world, have been remade."[3] Marina Sitrin and Dario Azzelini observe the following of Occupy and other movements of the squares:

> A key piece of the taking and using of space is that the movements are not doing it as a strategic holding, an occupation with a demand, such that when the demand is met then the occupation ends, as with traditional factory, school, or even political office occupations. The new movements' occupations are not pointed upward at institutional power, but across at one another, immediately creating alternatives and a new form of value production.[4]

But while more than an event, the occupation was still largely a performance. No U.S. occupation managed to endure for longer than two months, and the places in which they took shape — city parks — weren't capable of sustaining life in the long term. But did this make the occupations any less real? In W.J.T. Mitchell's formulation, the tents of Occupy "symbolized the manifestation of a long-term resolve," which is to say, they had their own reality but — at least to begin with — that reality couldn't be teased

---

[3] Jodi Dean, "Occupation as Political Form," *Occupy Everything*, April 12, 2012, http://occupyeverything.org/2012/occupation-as-political-form/.

[4] Sitrin and Azzelini, *Occupying Language*, 59.

apart from their symbolic function.[5] The aesthetics and the politics of Occupy were both of a total character.

Many commentators have remarked upon the art-like "feel" of the various occupations. In his ethnography of Occupy Wall Street (OWS), Mick Taussig observed: "This is not only a struggle about income disparity and corporate control of democracy. It is about the practice of art, too, including the art of being alive."[6] Gan Golan goes even further, arguing that Occupy was first and foremost a cultural movement: "From day one, rather than seeking to argue its case with policy prescriptions, it ignited the popular imagination with a vision of the impossible made real, expressed through posters (the ballerina atop the bull) and short films (Anonymous's online videos) and then the massive art explosion that followed."[7] Caron Atlas suggests that it isn't surprising that creativity would play a leading role in this sort of activism: "after all, believing that another world is possible requires an imaginative leap."[8]

The origin myths of Occupy Wall Street — the initial Zucotti Park occupation — are myriad, some located in the realm of arts and culture and others in autonomous politics. Its wellspring lies somewhere between the two. Certainly, the role of *AdBusters* magazine, a "culture-jamming" enterprise dedicated to the subversion and redeployment of advertising culture and techniques, is well-documented. *Adbusters* blogged and tweeted the original call for 20,000 people to "#Occupy Wall Street / August 17th / Bring tent," and created the aforementioned poster of the ballerina dancing on the bull. Others trace the birth of OWS to 16 Beaver, an art space near Wall Street, where, as Yates McKee recalls, a group of artists, activists, writers, students, and

---

[5] William Mitchell, "Image, Space, Revolution: The Arts of Occupation," in Mitchell, Harcourt, and Taussig, *Occupy*, 106.

[6] Michael Taussig, "I'm So Angry I Made a Sign," in Mitchell, Harcourt, and Taussig, *Occupy*, 18.

[7] Gan Golan, "The Office of the People," in *Beyond Zuccotti Park: Freedom of Assembly and the Occupation of Public Space,* ed. Ron Shiffman (Oakland: New Village Press, 2012), 73.

[8] Caron Atlas, "Radical Imagination," in *Beyond Zuccotti Park*, 147.

organizers had gathered in the early summer of 2011 for a series of open seminars with George Caffentzis, Sylvia Federici (yes, that Sylvia Federici), and David Graeber on "debt and the commons," which took place alongside report backs on the recent uprisings in Tunisia, Egypt, Spain, and Greece.[9] These conversations were facilitated by long-time 16 Beaver organizers Ayreen Anastas and Rene Gabri, whose 2006 social practice project Camp Campaign, McKee suggests, "stands as an uncanny prophecy of a different kind of camp campaign that would unfurl several years later at Wall Street."[10]

In the month preceding the birth of OWS, a number of participants from the 16 Beaver conversations, including the Greek artist Georgia Sagri, attended an anti-austerity rally next to the iconic bull sculpture, organized by a coalition named New Yorkers Against Budget Cuts in Bowling Green.[11] Disappointed with what looked to be the usual single-issue focused rally, Sagri pushed for a strategic departure, arguing instead for a general assembly — the kind of wide-ranging, unscripted, radical consensus-making forum she'd recently experienced in Syntagma Square. She and the others migrated away from the larger group and began on the spot to plan the New York City General Assembly, beginning the process of occupying Wall Street that would ramp up on August 17 in response to the *Adbusters* call.

They were joined by a small group of anarchist activists also present at the rally, including theorist David Graeber, who in his own account foregrounds the autonomous political dimension of the action: "A small group of anarchists and other antiauthoritarians [...] effectively wooed everyone away from the planned march and rally to create a genuine democratic assem-

---

9 Yates McKee, *Strike Art: Contemporary Art and the Post-Occupy Condition* (London: Verso, 2016), 91–92.

10 Ibid., 82.

11 Andy Kroll, "How Occupy Wall Street Really Got Started," *Mother Jones*, October 17, 2017, http://www.motherjones.com/politics/2011/10/occupy-wall-street-international-origins.

bly, on basically anarchist principles."[12] The anarchist principles at work in Occupy, he asserts, were the refusal to accept the legitimacy of existing political institutions; the refusal to accept the legitimacy of the existing legal order; the refusal to create an internal hierarchy; the early adoption of a form of consensus-based direct democracy; and the embrace of prefigurative politics — "the genuine attempt to create the institutions of a new society in the shell of the old."[13]

One thing no one could deny who got within twenty feet of any occupation was the *affective* power of this particular blend of art and politics. The work of Lauren Berlant is key to understanding exactly why, particularly her essay "Cruel Optimism," which names "a relation of attachment to compromised conditions of possibility whose realization is discovered either to be impossible, sheer fantasy, or too possible, and toxic."[14] Cruel optimism aptly describes the affect of the 99% in the decade leading up to Occupy, a time when "ordinary Americans" persisted in their affective attachment to "what we call the good life, which is for so many a bad life that wears out the subjects who nonetheless, and at the same time, find their conditions of possibility within it."[15]

As Lisa Duggan argues, building on Berlant, this *cruel optimism* was married under neoliberal capitalism to a complementary relation of attachment, *optimistic cruelty,* which describes those "motivated to join or remain among the 1% by any means necessary."[16] Duggan locates a primary locus of "optimistic cruelty" in the work and reception of Ayn Rand, whose novels "provide a libidinal fantasy life for the would-be heroic entrepreneur

---

12 David Graeber, "Occupy Wall Street's Anarchist Roots," *Al Jazeera,* November 30, 2011, https://www.aljazeera.com/opinions/2011/11/30/occupy-wall-streets-anarchist-roots.

13 Ibid.

14 Lauren Berlant, "Cruel Optimism," in *The Affect Theory Reader,* eds. Melissa Gregg and Gregory J. Seigworth (Durham: Duke University Press, 2010), 94.

15 Ibid., 97.

16 Lisa Duggan, "Optimistic Cruelty," *Social Text,* January 15, 2013, http://socialtextjournal.org/periscope_article/optimistic-cruelty/.

who eschews empathy and collectivity on the path to pure creative achievement."[17] She calls attention to the widespread promulgation of Rand's texts and ideas by neoliberal politicians and government officials such as Paul Ryan and Alan Greenspan, suggesting that Rand's fiction provides another "structure of feeling, a moralized and libidinal politics of joyful greediness in the face of scarcity and conflict."[18]

The signage at Occupy Wall Street signaled a break with all of this: GIVE A DAMN. PEOPLE OVER PROFIT / I LOVE HUMANITY – LET'S FIGURE THIS SHIT OUT TOGETHER / ARE WE REALLY GOING TO LET A BUNCH OF GREEDY SELFISH FOOLS DO IN THIS WHOLE PLANET? / I'M SO ANGRY THAT I MADE A SIGN. It took on a truth value precisely because it described a shift away from neoliberal affect that was in fact already underway: a "bad" feeling was beginning to emerge about the previously lionized entrepreneur, accompanied by a "good" feeling about collectivity. These affective shifts extended to the rampant privatization of public space and the retaking of that space for conversations and activities not wholly determined by the market. This aesthetico-affective dimension of Occupy might account for the participants' resistance to drawing up explicit demands and their oft-expressed desire to extend the moment of manifestation by putting off the fixing of political form — to keep the feeling alive.

Raymond Williams defines a "structure of feeling" as constituting the present of lived social experience, rather than the fixed, explicit, and already known relationships, institutions, formations, and positions that frame that experience, which are always consigned to the past. Like Castoriadis, Williams is critical of the reduction of the social to fixed forms, arguing that structures of feeling "do not have to await definition, classification, or rationalization before they exert palpable pressures and set effective limits on experience and on action."[19] Perhaps most

---

17 Ibid.
18 Ibid.
19 Raymond Williams, *Marxism and Literature* (Oxford: Oxford University Press, 1977), 132.

importantly for us, he suggests that structures of feeling first appear in a recognizable form in art and literature, where "the true social content is in a significant number of cases of this present and affective kind, which cannot without loss be reduced to belief-systems, institutions, or explicit general relationships."[20]

Indeed, changes in artistic forms and conventions "are often among the very first indications that such a new structure [of feeling] is forming."[21] Suggesting that this may in fact be the true source of the "specializing categories of 'the aesthetic,' 'the arts,' and 'imaginative literature,'" he maps a temporal dimension onto art's autonomy. But rather than tying that dimension to a post-revolutionary future, as Adorno and Marcuse do, he asserts that art is different from other discourses because of its connection to the emerging *present,* its alignment with instituting rather than instituted or one-day-to-be-instituted society. He argues that we need "on the one hand to acknowledge (and welcome) the specificity of these elements — specific feelings, specific rhythms — and yet [also] to find ways of recognizing their specific kinds of sociality," the ways that art puts us in touch with a society in the process of becoming. By doing so, we can prevent "that extraction from social experience which is conceivable only when social experience itself has been categorically (and at root historically) reduced" to systems and structures alone.[22]

One might say that this is what the social turn in art in the late nineties/early oughts preceding Occupy was all about: making art's specific forms of sociality the content of the art itself. As we've seen, the social forms highlighted most often in these practices were collaboration (forms of association that take place in and through creative practice), improvisation (emphasizing the mutuality of individual and collective creativity), and non-capitalist exchanges or distributive processes (free things, food, information, and skills).

---

20 Ibid. 133.
21 Ibid.
22 Ibid.

Derided in some quarters as mere conviviality, such practices at their best performed what sociologist George Simmel calls *sociability*, the distillation out of the realities of social life of "the pure essence of association, of the associative process as a value and a satisfaction."[23] For Simmel, sociability is fundamentally about "good form," defined in terms of the "mutual self-definition" of participants, and it produces radically democratic interactions: "It is a game in which one 'acts' as though all were equal." Sociability, and art that has sociability as its medium, allow us to experiment with equality and freedom and to experience their meanings, even if they don't (yet) exist in our social structures. When politicized, sociability becomes solidarity — that "good feeling" about collectivity (relentlessly hammered at by neoliberal thought and practice) which motivates and enables groups to struggle.

As Kester notes in a 2015 essay, "This isn't to say that there aren't numerous 'social art' projects that are based on simplistic, de-politicized concepts of community. However, if these projects are problematic, it's not because they seek to engage in a concrete manner with the world outside the gallery or museum, or rely on processes of consensually based action. It's because they have a naïve or non-existent understanding of power and the nature of resistance."[24] But as Greg Sholette argued a decade before Occupy in "Some Call It Art: From Imaginary Autonomy to Autonomous Collectivity," there also existed forms of relational art that did not "seek to insure art's usefulness to the liberal, corporate state but to offer up a model of political and economic self-valorization that is applicable for social transformation in the broadest sense."[25] He cites the practices of specific

---

23 Georg Simmel, *On Individuality and Social Forms* (Chicago: University of Chicago Press, 1972), 128.

24 Grant Kester, "On the Relationship between Theory and Practice in Socially Engaged Art," *A Blade of Grass,* July 29, 2015, https://abladeofgrass.org/fertile-ground/on-the-relationship-between-theory-and-practice-in-socially-engaged-art/.

25 Gregory Sholette, "Some Call It Art: From Imaginary Autonomy to Autonomous Collectivity," *Subsol,* http://subsol.c3.hu/subsol_2/contributors3/

groups to back this claim, including Temporary Services, the Yes Men, and Ultra Red, who while "self-identified as art," organized themselves "into collective units of production, distribution, and intervention/disruption." It was groups like these who found their way to Occupy.

That the art practices that preceded and helped to spark Occupy had more political content than mere "conviviality" is underscored by an anecdote related by Nato Thompson, who had organized the *Living as Form* exhibition and conference, which provided an overview of socially engaged art from 1991 to 2011, just prior to the start of Occupy Wall Street. Thompson recalls how, at the very last panel of the conference, which took place in Manhattan, "the audience and artists speaking decided to forego the talk and instead head down to the occupation and begin organizing [...] the connections between the socially engaged work and the need for a radical encounter and contestation with the powers of global finance and control were apparent."[26] Art and politics could not stay in their separate spheres of influence once the process of undoing those spheres — of "occupying everything" — had begun. "Foregoing the talk" becomes in this instance, not the jettisoning of art or theory for "life" nor even for "politics," as Adorno feared, but a recognition of the fact that the questions and affects at the heart of these art practices were in that very moment on the move.

---

sholettetext.html.

26 Nato Thompson, "The Occupation of Wall Street Across Time and Space," *Transversal Texts*, October 2011, https://transversal.at/transversal/1011/thompson/en.

THIRTEENTH LETTER

On Autonomy and Emplacement

Dear A,

For months after the Occupy LA encampment in front of City Hall was razed, my two-year-old would joyfully shout "The Occupation!" whenever we drove by. Did she remember it as the place where she and her babysitting coop pals spent sunny weekend afternoons rolling down a grassy hill? Where a kind stranger offered up a carton of strawberries? The place her parents talked about with a mixture of wonder and anxiety, like it was something important, something precious? I'll never know what exactly prompted these eruptions, and by now she's forgotten, but I always took pleasure in this cry of recognition, which momentarily replaced the seat of governance with a memory of that other, brief-lived site of self-governance.

For Michael Rios, it was the physical "emplacement" of Occupy New York that accounted for its ability to bring art and politics into meaningful relation, "creating an event and mobilizing a public through art and symbolism; occupying a 'privately owned public plaza' as a legal right through a regulatory loophole; and procuring an uncanny scene of pitched tents in the middle of a corporate landscape."[1] As we have seen, artists

---

1 Michael Rios, "Emplacing Democratic Design," in *Beyond Zuccotti Park: Freedom of Assembly and the Occupation of Public Space*, ed. Ron Shiffman

played a role in "immediately defin[ing] these spaces as different, separate, and autonomous," through visual means (DIY signs and screen painting coexisting with Mark de Suvero's towering red "Joie de Vivre" statue, installed in the park five years earlier as if in anticipation of the movement to come), and through performance and social practice. "The artistic spectacle that is Liberty Square [Zucotti Park] puts anyone entering the space on alert," Golan asserts, "declaring loudly that 'if you enter here, know that this space does not abide by the same rules as the rest of society.' You are allowed to change it, make it yours, and allow yourself to become someone else."[2]

For me, this meant raising a rainbow banner made by my husband and a comrade that spelled out HORIZONTALIDAD, and standing under it reading aloud first-person accounts of the 2001 uprising in Argentina; bringing our babysitting coop down to the occupation on Saturdays and Sundays, so that no one had to be left out; and fast and furious "Banks got bailed out! We got sold out!" marches out of the encampment into the city, unpermitted and always stalked by police (though not, until the end, riot cops), from which we returned to an occupation that always felt a little bigger, a little freer than before. It meant, one day, turning out of the parking lot with babe-in-stroller to find myself comically at the very front of one of these marches, like Charlie Chaplin with his red flag in *Modern Times,* running to stay abreast of it so we wouldn't get mowed down. And it meant for two months always to be thinking, at work or at home (because I didn't sleep at Occupy, wasn't an organizer, but still felt — was encouraged to feel — like I could do something to help), what can we, what can I do to keep this going?

The fact that Occupy *had* a place, *was* a place, was incredibly important; it staked out a territory, half-real, half-imaginary, that was organized according to non-capitalist principles, where people could think and talk about what had been done to them and what they wanted to do about it — a place that at the time,

---

(Oakland: New Village Press, 2012), 139.
2   Golan, "Office of the People," in *Beyond Zuccotti Park,* ed. Shiffman, 73.

with the almost complete privatization of public space (literal and imaginative) that had been achieved under neoliberalism, literally felt like it didn't exist. And then it did. "We found each other," Naomi Klein said in her speech to Occupy Wall Street. "That sentiment captures the beauty of what is being created here. A wide-open space (as well as an idea so big it can't be contained by any space) for all the people who want a better world to find each other."³ McKee, who performs a detailed analysis of Occupy Wall Street's emplacement in *Strike Art,* insists we acknowledge the difference of this particular "wide-open space," which was not "merely a place of gathering or protest, but rather a collective apparatus working to [...] 'reterritorialize' a nominally public space as a communal life-support zone resistant to both the market and state-sanctioned versions of public assembly."⁴

Emplacement is a hallmark of autonomous politics in general (think squats, punk houses, communes), precisely because it foregrounds an everyday life experience of radical collaborative making and remaking that does not or cannot take place in the larger society as of yet. It's the future projected onto the present, the temporal dimension spatialized, a possibility opened up within conditions of impossibility. It creates *enclaves,* which Fredric Jameson describes as "something like a foreign body within the social: [...] they remain as it were momentarily beyond the reach of the social and testify to its political powerlessness, at the same time that they offer a space in which new wish images of the social can be elaborated and experimented on."⁵

And yet, Occupy's location in urban parks, while rendering its all-encompassing demand to start everything over highly visible, also made it especially vulnerable to repression. And

---

3 Naomi Klein, "Occupy Wall Street: The Most Important Thing in the World Now," *The Nation,* October 6, 2011, http://www.thenation.com/article/163844/occupy-wall-street-most-important-thing-world-now.

4 Yates McKee, *Strike Art: Contemporary Art and the Post-Occupy Condition* (London: Verso, 2016), 102.

5 Fredric Jameson, *Archaeologies of the Future: The Desire Called Utopia and Other Science Fictions* (London: Verso, 2005), 16.

the movement's emphasis on prefiguration, arguably stemming from its origins in art and anarchism, was the subject of much criticism. Graeber in particular was excoriated by Marxist theorist Andrew Kliman for espousing what Kliman called a politics of "make-believe," insofar as Graeber conceived of the occupation as a direct action that at its core did not—like a protest—demand freedom, but encouraged participants to act as if they were *already* free, already creating the world they wish to see. Kliman observes, "You're not free, but you make believe that you are. You can't make history 'under self-selected circumstances,' but you make believe that you can. [...] It's a refusal to recognize facts."[6] This refusal is dangerous, he argues, because "acting as if you were already free is [...] no solution at all if you're forced into a confrontation. Graeber leaves us with this: pretend that things are different than they really are, which provokes a reaction, which in turn leads to a situation in which force decides. You've opened up a space of autonomy, until you haven't."[7]

Certainly force did seem to decide in the case of Occupy, with the Homeland Security/FBI/police-coordinated eviction of Zuccotti Park and other Occupy encampments two months in, and over 7,000 arrests during the course of the short-lived movement. Even Graeber concedes, at the end of the interview Kliman is citing, that "he doesn't think we can do without confrontation of any kind," while stipulating that "the exact mix of withdrawal and confrontation cannot be predicted." This question—of where and when to invest in creating an autonomous space and where and when to engage in contestation, was a central one for Occupy and remains a central one for all autonomous politics. Where—and when—Occupy was most successful, it got this balance right, for instance in Oakland, where

---

6 Andrew Kliman, "The Make-Believe World of David Graeber," *Marxist Humanities Initiative,* April 13, 2012, http://www.marxisthumanistinitiative.org/alternatives-to-capital/the-make-believe-world-of-david-graeber.html.

7 Ibid.

occupiers marched forth from a robust encampment to shut down the port. Where it was less so, for instance, in Los Angeles, more of a hippy love-in vibe prevailed after those first heady days, a love that despite vocal opposition was also extended to the police surrounding the camp, who were welcomed as part of the 99%.

The necessary relation between negation and creation is aptly described by those who occupied UC campuses as part of the anti-austerity movement of 2009–2010, a number of whom eventually migrated to Occupy Oakland:

> The real dialectic is between negation and experimentation: acts of resistance and refusal which also enable an exploration of new social relations, new uses of space and time. These two poles can't be separated out, since the one passes into the other with surprising swiftness. Without confrontation, experiments risk collapsing back into the existing social relations that form their backdrop — they risk becoming mere lifestyle or culture [...] but to the extent that any experiment really attempts to take control of space and time and social relations, it will necessarily entail an antagonistic relation to power.[8]

In the case of Occupy, police repression shifted the focus and energy of the antagonistic relation to power onto holding the space itself, rather than using it as a base from which to challenge the status quo. The prefigurative aspect of the encampments was similarly overwhelmed by the intense demands of life on the street. As Wendy E. Brawer and Brennan S. Cavanaugh recount in their participant ethnography of Zuccotti: "The area that was covered with a forest of cardboard signs, facing One Liberty Plaza, gave way eventually to tents. By the end, everything gave

---

[8] "The Introduction from After the Fall: Communiqués from Occupied California," *libcom,* February 16, 2010, https://libcom.org/library/introduction-after-fall-communiqu%C3%A9s-occupied-california.

way to the tents."⁹ Interviewees who lived in the encampments talk about clashes between more recently dispossessed occupiers and the chronically homeless who found their way there; the dystopic dynamics that found concrete expression in the geography of the camps, reinforcing class divisions; and the attrition of middle-class occupiers as soon as it became clear exactly how overwhelming the need for free services and a safe place to sleep on the streets of Manhattan and other U.S. cities actually was.

Given these dynamics, it's not surprising (though certainly not inevitable) that the occupations would "give way" to tents, and the encampments, once stripped of political meaning, would be targeted by authorities citing concerns about safety, hygiene, the presence of children. After a coordinated police sweep of the main occupations in mid-November 2011, the movement dissipated and the over eight hundred encampments disappeared, though autonomous actions continued on with Occupy Sandy, the emergency response to Hurricane Sandy, and Rolling Jubilee, a strike debt project, and Occupy's systemic critique continued to course through our language and politics, with the rhetoric of the 99% and the 1% taking hold of the general discourse.

That Occupy did not end capitalism, that there has been no change to our system of government, nor even to the corruption of that system, does not mean that it failed. To the contrary: It provided a space for social imagining that jumpstarted the process of undoing the forty years of antisocial imagination that preceded it. The decade following has seen the rebirth of union organizing (particularly teachers' strikes, with their comprehensive demands), and the spread of tenant unions and anti-gentrification efforts. The successive explosions of the Black Lives Matter, Standing Rock, and Me Too movements (so rapid as to be considered part of the same "moment"), have shown just how far and deep the radical imaginary goes.

---

9   Wendy E. Brawer and Brennan S. Cavanaugh, "Being There," in *Beyond Zuccotti Park*, ed. Shiffman, 57.

Standing Rock in particular demonstrated the power of emplacement, hearkening back to previous reverse-occupations and politicized encampments initiated by the American Indian Movement in the 1970s, as well as indigenous traditions of self-governance going back centuries that continue to pose a radical challenge to the nation state, private property, and the desecration of the environment. "Indigenous freedom was, and is a place," Nick Estes argues, and "for a moment it took place in the #NoDAPL camps."[10] As compared to Occupy's practice of political disobedience in civic parks, the Standing Rock occupation went a step further — make that many steps further — into the radical imaginary. The #NoDAPL camps and determined blockades of pipeline construction were sustained through indigenous communal and spiritual traditions that, under the banner "Water is Life," mounted a radical challenge to the principle and practice of endless expansion upheld by capitalism and the state and foregrounded the absolute necessity of self-limitation — of "being a good relative to the water, land, and animals, not to mention the human world."[11]

---

10 Nick Estes, *Our History Is the Future: Standing Rock versus the Dakota Access Pipeline, and the Long Tradition of Indigenous Resistance* (London: Verso, 2019), 253.

11 Ibid., 21.

FOURTEENTH LETTER

On New Forms of Autonomous Politics in Our Era and a New Mode of Instituting

Dear A,

That autonomy is a generative lens through which to view the politics of our moment is further borne out by the practices of Black Lives Matter and Me Too. In both movements we find a familiar emphasis on the mutually constituting relationship between individual and collective, the central role of affect and aesthetics in bringing about social transformation, and the need for a radical revaluation of all values. This last is especially important, because while there have been other significant national and transnational political formations within the last decade, such as the Never Again movement against gun violence and the Youth Climate Strike movement, these have been largely focused (so far) on changing national and international policy within a liberal democratic framework.

The Black Lives Matter Movement (BLM) came into being amidst an outpouring of feeling—specifically *grief*—over the murder of a seventeen-year-old Black youth, Trayvon Martin, at the hands of a racist vigilante, a feeling that was formalized and politicized via a hashtag: #BlackLivesMatter. In many ways, BLM was about the right to *have* that feeling, to mourn, to feel sad, to be moved, to not move on, to refuse to move on, to grow angry and move on but in a different direction, away from all that is and toward everything that could be.

One of BLM's origin stories begins with two Facebook posts by West Coast community organizers and BLM cofounders Alicia Garza and Patrisse Cullors on the day Zimmerman was acquitted.[1] *Black people I love you,* typed Garza, *I love us. Our lives matter.* To which Cullors responded: *declaration: black bodies will no longer be sacrificed for the rest of the world's enlightenment. i am done. i am so done. trayvon, you are loved infinitely. #blacklivesmatter.* A third cofounder, Opal Tometi, reached out to Garza and Cullors and began organizing a social media presence around Cullors's hashtag. By the following Monday, she had changed her Facebook status to *Started Working at Black Lives Matter.*

Let's pause for a moment to think about how hashtags work — and how quickly. The form of the hashtag allows for the articulation of both a singularity, the message preceding it, and a collectivity, the shared concern expressed in the tag itself. Hashtags are a lazy — in a strictly formal sense — form of organizing that can reach millions of people in the time it takes to plan a protest march of a few hundred. In the case of #BlackLivesMatter, the message attached to the hashtag couples an insistence on holding police accountable for specific lives, via the naming of individual victims and the circumstances of their murders, with a continuous tally of police murders and subsequent acquittals that accretes into an undeniable truth: that Black lives *don't* matter in this society, that the entire structure of society is predicated on their not mattering, and that this structure must be radically transformed.

BLM also owed its rise to the smartphone video documentation of police brutality and its online dissemination via the technologies of Facebook and Twitter, which were relatively

---

[1] MSNBC, "Queerness on the Front Lines of #BlackLivesMatter | Original | msnbc," *YouTube*, February 20, 2015, https://www.youtube.com/watch?v=oYHs9jIH-00.

new at that time, and which allowed for widespread witnessing of brutal acts as well as viewers' responses to them. The fact that this dissemination occurred via "sharing" as opposed to broadcasting is crucial. For all its co-optation by platform capitalism, the sharing function does create a condition of mutuality: One cannot silently witness, one must respond (and even if one doesn't respond, the demand is made). The videos existed on a continuum with the "body rhetoric" of protesters in the street, to use Frederick Hayman's term, who created new gestures of dissent by appropriating the last words and/or movements of Black men gunned down by police — Eric Garner ("I can't breathe"), Mike Brown ("Hands up, don't shoot") — and resurrected by the body politic.[2] What has by now become a "spectacle of black death" through endless repetition, in that moment achieved a redistribution of the sensible that made anti-Black police brutality visible to many non-Black people for the first time. That the murders were "reported" by community members present on the scene, by anguished friends and loved ones, effected a radical departure from the usual anti-Black, pro-police script of broadcast media.

The police murder of Mike Brown in 2014 again sparked massive protests under the sign (and signs) of BLM in Ferguson, Missouri, and all over the country; Freddie Gray's fatal "rough ride" in a police van in Baltimore, Maryland, eight months later would have a similar effect. *Uprising* is a better way of describing these events, as protests were in each instance accompanied by riots pushing beyond the current conditions of possibility. As Joshua Clover argues, the riot "is the experience of surplus. Surplus danger, surplus information, surplus military gear. Surplus emotion." His invocation of affect is not incidental: "Riots were once known as 'emotions,' a history still visible in the French word: *émeute*."[3]

---

2   Franklyn S. Haiman, "The Rhetoric of the Streets: Some Legal and Ethical Considerations," *Quarterly Journal of Speech* 53, no. 2 (1967): 99–114.

3   Joshua Clover, *Riot. Strike. Riot: The New Era of Uprisings* (London: Verso, 2016), 1.

In the present day, Clover argues, the riot increasingly features as "the central figure of political antagonism," part of a larger category of what he calls "circulation struggles," which includes the occupation, the blockade, and "at the far end," the commune.[4] Riots, with their tactics of vandalism and looting, call into question the organization of society around private property and the market — going "too far," for liberal society, in the struggle to get free. That there was no pitting of "peaceful protest" against "violent riots" within the rhetoric of the movement itself underscores the totality of BLM's demand and its willingness to transgress the limits of acceptable dissent.

Another tactic employed by BLM was that of being a leaderless, or in Garza and Cullors's words, "leaderful" movement, which they argue creates "much more room for collaboration, for expansion, for building power."[5] In their analysis, informed by Black feminism, leaderful movements encourage continuous creativity and prevent leadership from being organized around "one notion of Blackness." The Black transfeminist orientation of BLM's founders also played a role in their refusal to organize behind a single charismatic leader (e.g., Martin Luther King Jr.): "When a movement full of leaders from the margins gets underway," they observe, "it makes the connections between social ills, it rejects the compromise and respectability politics of the past, and it opens up new political space for radical visions of what this nation can truly become."[6]

As the BLM *organization* (as opposed to movement) took shape, it drew on already existing and thus more legible forms of rhetoric and organization, from the "Freedom Ride" bringing busloads of activists to support Ferguson activism in the wake of Brown's murder, to the member chapter formation it subsequently adopted and the Movement for Black Lives policy

---

4 Ibid., 31.
5 Alicia Garza and Patrisse Cullors-Brignac, "Celebrating MLK Day: Reclaiming Our Movement Legacy," *Huffington Post,* March 20, 2015, https://www.huffpost.com/entry/reclaiming-our-movement-l_b_6498400.
6 Ibid.

agenda it currently supports. But Black Lives Matter persists as something more than these institutions, because the demand it makes can only be truly met by an entirely new mode of instituting. The prevalence of prison and police abolition as a long-term goal within the movement, and its embrace of "non-reformist" criminal justice reforms in the meantime, is a testament to that fact (and here BLM draws on the work of longstanding abolitionist organizations such as Critical Resistance, cofounded by professors Ruth Wilson Gilmore and Angela Davis, formerly a Black Panther). Another indication of BLM's radical horizon is the way we continue to pour into the streets, murder after murder, city after city, in a Great Refusal, no longer waiting for the system to playact its response.

For the Me Too movement, the hashtag was also constitutive. It first appeared in 2017, in the midst of a series of high-profile sexual assault cases brought against Hollywood actor and comedian Bill Cosby by (ultimately) sixty women across multiple generations. And while its origins are obscure, Hollywood actress Alyssa Milano is credited with making it go viral when she retweeted a screenshot texted to her by a friend that read: *If all the women who have been sexually harassed or assaulted wrote 'me too' as a status, it might give people a sense of the magnitude of the problem, to which she added, if you've been sexually assaulted or harassed, write 'me too' as a reply to this tweet.* By morning, Milano had received 55,000 replies, and a month and a half later, #MeToo had been posted 85 million times.[7]

Each #MeToo post — many of which gave specific accounts of assault and/or harassment — marked the moment a survivor linked their individual story up to a collective experience, and it did, as predicted, give a sense of the magnitude of the problem, almost to the point of paralysis (do you remember those first few days, scrolling, scrolling, scrolling?). But it did something

---

7 Nadja Sayej, "Alyssa Milano on the #MeToo Movement: 'We're Not Going to Stand for It Any More,'" *The Guardian,* December 1, 2017, https://www.theguardian.com/culture/2017/dec/01/alyssa-milano-mee-too-sexual-harassment-abuse.

else as well, which was already happening in the legal battles against Cosby, and not long after, Hollywood producer Harvey Weinstein. It pinpointed particular nodes of domination and exploitation as they radiated out from powerful men through their networks and influences and tracked them through time.

Lisa Duggan criticizes this aspect of Me Too as being at least "one part neoliberal publicity stunt," inasmuch as "accusations are focused through the press primarily on bad individuals, rather than structures of power, and because the mode of accountability is primarily corporate investigation and firing."[8] She sees this as an individualistic approach that participates in the "privatization of feminism" and connects Me Too to the sex panics of old.[9] But while certainly corporate responses to Me Too have attempted to quickly deal with the problem by firing predatory CEOs (or just as often, putting them on six months leave and then bringing them back after the uproar dies down), I would argue that Me Too has actually taken a left and not a right turn from its most immediate mainstream predecessor, "lean in feminism."

For Me Too's power lies in its challenge to individualistic thinking. One woman can be disbelieved, but six or seven — or sixty, as in the Cosby case — are harder to discount, especially when those women span generations. In this way, Me Too explodes the conventional he said/she said narrative that in times past so often resulted in the victim being disbelieved and pilloried for sullying the "good name" of her victimizer. A pattern emerges that cannot be unseen — and not just of bad behavior by one individual, but of systems of peonage that have aided and abetted that individual in their actions for years. What's more it denaturalizes sexual exploitation and makes it visible everywhere, with the hashtag continually expanding Me Too's horizons to take on sexual assault and harassment not only in other workplaces but also on the street and in the home. Most

---

8 Lisa Duggan, "The Full Catastrophe," *Bully Bloggers*, August 18, 2018 https://bullybloggers.wordpress.com/2018/08/18/the-full-catastrophe/.
9 Ibid.

importantly, this is all brought to light by intergenerational solidarity among women — and others suffering from gender-based or exacerbated oppression and exploitation — which aims at the roots of a patriarchy firmly anchored in their separation and antagonism.

Me Too's radical horizon was further shaped through the intervention of BIPOC feminist activists, who made sure that the pre-hashtag organizing around the phrase "me too" begun a decade earlier by Tarana Burke, an activist working with young women of color, was acknowledged and folded into the contemporary moment. In the process of developing a practice of "empowerment through empathy," rooted in her own experience as a sexual assault survivor, Burke had created a "Me Too" virtual meeting place on MySpace as far back as 2006, where the young women she worked with could share their stories. Her history of organizing against sexual violence among marginalized women helped push the Me Too movement further in the direction of a systemic critique (while also linking two different "generations" of internet activism). As Burke sees it:

> #MeToo was a moment in history that elevated the Me Too movement, that amplified it and sent it off into the stratosphere and made it incredibly visible. But if we consider #MeToo the movement, then we will only define Me Too in the ways that the mainstream media has, and then we will only ever be looking for who's the next case? Who's the next person who's going to get Me Too'd? [...] I believe in vision, and movements are carried by vision. If we have the limited vision that the hashtag gives us, then we won't ever make the kind of progress that's necessary to actually look like we might end sexual violence.[10]

---

10 Nicole Carroll, "Tarana Burke on the Power of Empathy: The Building Block of the Me Too Movement," *USA Today,* August 19, 2020, https://www.usatoday.com/in-depth/life/women-of-the-century/2020/08/19/tarana-burke-me-too-movement-19th-amendment-women-of-century/5535976002/. My emphasis.

While it has spawned reformist organizations such as Times Up, Me Too, like Black Lives Matter — the hashtag, the phrase, the feeling, the organizing — continues to function in excess of any given situation. It provides an interpretive lens, a filter for the streams of information we are constantly receiving, organizing our thoughts as much as our actions. Most of all, it functions as connective tissue from case to case, place to place, era to era, creating cognitive and affective linkages that, even once a particular social media storm is over, prevent power relations from settling back down into their former configuration, leaving them charged and destabilized by the revaluation (of men and women, power and nonpower, predation and survivorship) that has taken place.

We must acknowledge, of course, that there are social media algorithms at work designed to prevent us from organizing our thoughts and actions in the service of anything but capital. And the fact that the #MeToo hashtag was at least to begin with so strongly identified with the travails of Hollywood actresses warrants Duggan's — and Burke's — suspicious eye toward any actual remedies. Nonetheless the specter of "being me-too-ed" continues to haunt the social landscape precisely because it cannot truly be "fixed" except through a complete transvaluation of who speaks, who is heard, and who is believed. Black Lives Matter and Me Too moved and continue to move because they are a new mode of instituting that cannot be contained by the old institutions; they both deploy and transcend existing social media formats and organizational models and even ways of taking to the street, in the case of BLM. They're of this world and of another, better one: the world they bring into being with the totality of their demands.

FIFTEENTH LETTER

On Communization and/ as Autonomy

Dear A:

Let's take a look at another instance of the autonomy project in our moment, which has something in common, perhaps, with the "tendencies" that emerged from the ultra-left journals of yore, such as *Socialisme ou Barbarie* or *Correspondence*. This is communization, a tendency which, for that matter, isn't all that new — it first arose in the aftermath of 1968 and found an early manifestation in Autonomia — but is newly relevant. French in origin, its current incarnation largely resides in the tracts and journals produced by anonymous collectives beginning in the oughts: "The Call" by Tiqqun/Invisible Committee (French), *The Coming Insurrection* and subsequent texts by the Invisible Committee, and various writings by Théorie Communiste (French) and Endnotes (Anglo-U.S.). But it had a galvanizing effect on the California university tuition protests of 2009–2010, Occupy, and other movements of the squares, and continues to intersect with today's struggles in meaningful ways.

Communization seeks to answer the perennial question facing communist thought and organizing: How do we get from here to there? It does so by rejecting the notion of a necessary *transition* from capitalism to communism, a post-revolutionary period during which, having fought for and taken hold of production and the state, the proletariat would initiate the transition from socialism to full communism and the state would wither away. By contrast, the theory (and practice) of communization holds that the revolution does not come first, and communism after; revolution happens *through* the production of communism, either via self-organizing activities that multiply into full-blown insurrections or by assaults on capitalist categories such as "exchange, money, commodities, the existence of separate enterprises, the state and — most fundamentally — wage labour and the working class itself."[1] Communization thus makes an important break with the *temporality* inherent in the notion of a revolutionary transition, a break which puts the class struggle — or the struggle *against* class — on the same temporal plane and in touch with other struggles, a development in contemporary Marxist thought that has enormous potential.

In this letter, I home in on the Invisible Committee and Endnotes as two distinct currents within the communization tendency. "It's not a question of fighting for communism," says the Invisible Committee. "What matters is the communism that is lived *in the fight itself.*" IC tracts strive always to present a vision not of what could happen in the future, but of what is in the process of happening in the now. This is the true nature of clairvoyance, they maintain, citing Deleuze in 1968 ("It was a 'phenomenon of clairvoyance: a society suddenly saw what it contained that was intolerable and also saw the possibility of something else") and Benjamin as well ("Clairvoyance is the vision of that which is taking form. [...] Perceiving exactly what is taking place is more decisive than knowing the future in advance.").[2] Their writing thus remains purposefully in the realm of praxis, of lucidity without total elucidation, and has a distinctly poetic

---

[1] Endnotes, "Communisation and Value Form Theory: Introduction," *Endnotes* 2: "Misery and the Value Form" (2010), https://endnotes.org.uk/issues/2/en/endnotes-communisation-and-value-form-theory.

[2] The Invisible Committee, *Now,* trans. Robert Hurley (South Pasadena: Semiotexte, 2017), 86.

quality, a *poietic* quality — for to see clearly, they argue, means "being able to apprehend forms."[3]

It also has an affective quality, performing a call to and for solidarity across struggles. In contrast to "the pioneers of the workers' movement [who] were able to find each other in the workshop, then in the factory," IC argues, contemporary struggles have "the whole of social space in which to find each other. […] We have our hostility to this civilization for drawing lines of solidarity and of battle on a global scale."[4] For me, this was what made reading IC texts as they came out — in 2004, 2009, 2014, and 2017 — a meaningful experience. They articulated a politics that saw reinforcing potential in the struggles of the moment, which had capitalism but not only capitalism in their sights, and took joy in an unfolding "we" that was not amorphous so much as unstoppably morphing.

Describing it as the "we" of a position rather than a group, IC foregrounds its radical creativity, drawing on historical parallels: "It borrows sudden force from the Black Panthers, collective dining halls from the German *Autonomen,* tree houses and the art of sabotage from the British neo-Luddites, the careful choice of words from radical feminists, mass self-reductions from the Italian autonomists, and armed joy from the 2 June Movement."[5] It is a "we" that takes on the "I" of neoliberal individualism, formulating, like other autonomisms, an integral relationship between individual and collective: "We have been sold this lie: that what is most particular to us is what *distinguishes* us from the common. We experience the contrary: every singularity is felt in the *manner* and in the *intensity* with which a being brings into existence something common."[6]

IC's goal is communism, but their definition of communism is expansive; it is "the matrix of a meticulous, audacious assault

---

[3] Ibid., 152.
[4] The Invisible Committee, *The Coming Insurrection* (Los Angeles: Semiotext(e), 2009), 99.
[5] [Tiqqun/Invisible Committee], "The Call," *Anarchist Library,* https://theanarchistlibrary.org/library/anonymous-call.
[6] Ibid.

on domination. As a call and as a name for all worlds resisting imperial pacification, all solidarities irreducible to the reign of commodities, all friendships assuming the necessities of war."[7] It relies on the fundamental unit of the commune, understood in broad terms as "a pact to face the world together."[8] While the commune does have a territoriality, this too is fluidly defined: "A commune forms every time a few people, freed of their individual straitjackets, decide to rely only on themselves and measure their strength against reality. Every wildcat strike is a commune; every building occupied collectively and on a clear basis is a commune, the action committees of 1968 were communes, as were the slave maroons in the United States, or Radio Alice in Bologna in 1977."[9]

Of course their call would appeal to *me*, dear A, aren't I writing these letters to *you*? But the Invisible Committee's expansive definitions of the struggle at hand, the means for achieving it, who is to struggle and what is to be struggled against, are anathema to Endnotes, who argue that the call to solidarity that constitutes the major affective dimension of IC's tracts leads to voluntarism and simplification, "forstall[ing] any real grasp of the situation." The situation, as Endnotes see it, is that the revolutionary working class cannot (can no longer or perhaps could never) organize itself within capitalism to defeat capital but must instead attack the class relation itself and the category of value that upholds it, as in the circulation struggles of today's uprisings, which seek to disrupt the flow of commerce

Workers today, Endnotes argue, cannot lay claim to a shared "fictive identity," as did the historic workers' movement. That has been dissolved by the "corrosive character of capitalist social relations." They are united only by their separation by capital and are otherwise riven by a "sea of differential interests: those of women and men, young and old, 'white' and 'non-white' and

---

7 Ibid., 16.
8 The Invisible Committee, *To Our Friends*, trans. Robert Hurley (South Pasadena: Semiotext(e), 2015), 200.
9 The Invisible Committee, *The Coming Insurrection*, 102.

so on." While acknowledging that there are still moments when workers come together in struggle in a mode that interrupts their unity for capital, they no longer do so as a class, Endnotes argue, "for their class belonging is precisely what divides them. Instead, they come together under the name of some other unity — real democracy, the 99% — which appears to widen their capacity to struggle."[10] But this appearance is only a "foreshortened [critique] of an immense and terrible reality," Endnotes argues. The truth is that "ours is a society of strangers, engaged in a complex set of interactions. There is no one, no group or class, who controls these interactions. Instead, our blind dance is coordinated impersonally, through markets."[11]

Though dedicated to a systematic dialectics that does not unfold in obvious ways, cautioning that "the emergence of revolutions is, by its very nature, unpredictable," Endnotes do, in fact, seem to know what revolution should look like *in the end*. For instance, the revolutionary content of Occupy, in their analysis, lay solely in the conflict between middle- and working-class occupiers that arose in the encampments, while that of Ferguson could be found only in the disintegrating solidarity between black bourgeois activists and civil rights veterans and the rioting underclass ("Was class the rock on which race was to be wrecked, or its social root, by which it might be radicalised?"[12]). Certainly these dynamics are important to note, but shouldn't we also be paying attention to what *else* was going on, particularly when speaking of Ferguson? If not, we risk what George Ciccariello-Maher calls *dialectical betrayal*, "subsuming Blackness to the purportedly superior term of class."[13]

---

10 Endnotes, "A History of Separation: The Defeat of the Workers Movement," *Endnotes* 4: "Unity and Separation" (2015), https://endnotes.org.uk/issues/4/en/endnotes-the-defeat-of-the-workers-movement.

11 Ibid.

12 Endnotes, "Brown v. Ferguson," *Endnotes* 4: "Unity and Separation" (2015), https://endnotes.org.uk/issues/4/en/endnotes-brown-v-ferguson.

13 George Ciccariello-Maher, *Decolonizing Dialectics* (Durham: Duke University Press, 2017), 68.

In developing his concept of dialectical betrayal, Ciccariello-Maher cites Franz Fanon's critique of Jean-Paul Sartre, in which Fanon rejects Sartre's folding of the "subjective" experience of race into the more "objective" structure of class, and holds out for the possibility of Black people "living their blackness" and "creating a meaning" for themselves.[14] A "decolonized dialectics," Ciccariello-Maher argues, must bring the "banished zone of nonbeing" to which colonial subjects are consigned to bear on the social totality. "It is in the play between inside and outside, moreover, between aboveground and subterranean," he suggests, "that any and all determinism is lost, that 'the' dialectic collapses into many combative moments that nevertheless coalesce into broad oppositions, and that the reconciled horizon of the future remains that and nothing more: a horizon toward which to aim but never reach."[15]

Dialectics aside, Endnotes' attachment to the value form aligns with the autonomy project, since autonomy also concerns itself with forms of value (certainly Castoriadis for his part understands the value form to be one of the core meanings of capitalism). But while acknowledging that when people "make the leap" out of the community of capital, "they will have to figure out how to relate to each other and to the things themselves, in new ways," and that "there is no one way to do that," Endnotes overlooks what might *make* people take that leap: the forms and solidarities that belong to a different imaginary than that of capital. For why do people engage in revolutionary struggle, if not to create a new meaning for themselves out of what has been given to them? "Black" is one of those meanings. "The racialized poor," the term Endnotes prefers in its analysis of Ferguson, Baltimore, and so forth, is not. Notably, Fanon too describes a "leap" in *Black Skins, White Masks*—and though Ciccariello-Maher reads it as Fanon's articulation of a decolonized dialectic, it can also be read as a leap *into* autonomy:

---

14 Ibid.
15 Ibid., 159.

> I am not a prisoner of History…
> The real leap consists of introducing invention into life.
> In the world I am heading for, I am endlessly creating myself.
> I show solidarity with humanity provided I can go one step further.[16]

Autonomy is at the far end of Endnotes' project, to use Clover's turn of phrase, and at the near end of the Invisible Committee's. Endnotes acknowledges the latter when they dismiss IC's tracts as a mere dressing up of the "language of yesteryear," with their version of communization appearing "as a fashionable stand-in for slightly more venerable buzzwords such as 'autonomy.'"[17] But in seeking to engage with contemporary struggles, which are concerned with domination, but not domination by the value form alone, Endnotes also find themselves in the realm of autonomy. The social poetry of the IC is one way to navigate this territory, a decolonized dialectics another.

---

[16] Quoted in ibid., 70.
[17] Endnotes, "What Are We To Do?" in *Communization and Its Discontents*, ed. Noys, 24.

SIXTEENTH LETTER

On the Autonomy Project in Art Today, Which Is Everywhere and Nowhere

Dear A,

Some days I despair about contemporary art, don't you? Where is the art that's making its own rules, redistributing the sensible in ways that, however oblique, have the potential to spark the radical social imaginary? It is *everywhere* and *nowhere*. That is to say, it exists, but so long as art lies entombed in the market's gilded casket, slid neatly into place in the catacombs of global capitalism, it plays no role in the autonomy project. How do we bring it back to life?

In the past five years, there have been some notable attempts, and I begin this letter with a very quick sketch of the landscape in which these protests are taking place. Today's art market is dominated by the superstar phenomenon, in which, as Claire McAndrew observes, "a very small number of artists, and the galleries representing them, drive the bulk of sales value, while others struggle to survive."[1] McAndrew suggests this dynamic

---

1 Claire McAndrew, "Why the 'Superstar Economics' of the Art Market Is Its Biggest Threat," *Artsy*, November 27, 2017, https://www.artsy.net/article/artsy-editorial-superstar-economics-art-market-threat.

is due to the accumulation of wealth in the hands of a few, and their ability to promote the artists they collect to a wider audience. These lucky few largely fit the profile of "masters," demographically speaking. In 2017, only 13.7% of living artists represented by galleries in Europe and North America were women,[2] while a recent survey of the permanent collections of eighteen prominent art museums in the U.S. found that out of over ten thousand artists represented, 87% are male, and 85% are white.[3] It's really quite remarkable how little these numbers change — how consistently, for all its noisy trying, the art world fails to "do better." Indeed, there's so much consistency we'd have to be blind not to see that the art world's doing very well, thank you, it's (most) artists who are doing poorly — impotent, as Castoriadis would say, before their own creations. What is it that obscures this picture? And what keeps another one from forming?

Of course, the image that I began with, of art entombed in capitalism, is a heteronomy so normalized at this point as to be hardly worth mentioning. Art is a commodity like any other, or so we're told, and we're as powerless before that commodification as anybody else. But still we continue to have a notion, don't we, perhaps encapsulated in the term "art world," that art is not fully commodified, that it exists at least partially outside of capitalist processes and functions at least partially according to different laws, and that its autonomy has social and political effects.

Beginning with the publication of David Beech's *Art and Value* in 2015, and continuing with Nicholas Brown's *Autonomy: The Social Ontology of Art under Capitalism* (2019), we see growing support for this notion, and a reinvestment in its possibilities, within Marxist analysis. While Beech doesn't venture into

---

[2] Julia Halperin, "The Four Glass Ceilings: How Women Artists Get Stiffed at Every Stage of Their Careers," *Artnet,* December 15, 2017, https://news.artnet.com/market/art-market-study-1179317.

[3] See the National Museum of Women in the Arts website for a fuller picture: https://nmwa.org/advocate/get-facts.

the autonomy debates, he makes an argument for art's economic exceptionalism that clears the way for that discussion, positing a different pathway to commodification for art. The question, he says, is not whether art is economic — it is — nor whether art works are exchanged as commodities — they are — but what kinds of mechanisms are involved in art's production and exchange? If the division between a class of nonlaboring owners and a class of nonowner laborers is what sets capitalism apart, Beech argues, then the artist "who owns her own 'petty implements' and, unlike the wage labourer, continues to own the product she produces" constitutes an exception to capitalist social relations of production.[4]

Beech does not maintain that capitalism is absent from the art world, far from it: "Many of the most successful artists have taken on certain capitalist practices or, perhaps we could say, artists have learned from capitalists about how to run their studios, use marketing, produce their works more efficiently, and a range of other techniques."[5] But while opting out of capitalism is impossible, "many practices and forms of exchange within capitalism are not capitalistic in the strict sense of being engaged in for exchange, that is, to accumulate wealth. […] [A]rt is bound up with capitalism but does not conform to the capitalist mode of commodity production."[6] If "art has been commodified without being commodified," Beech maintains, then we must look to the "full variety of social mechanisms active in art's production and reproduction." And though his project does not take this next step, I will: Insofar as art making is not wholly determined by the movement of capital (though certainly affected by it), it constitutes a field of autonomy (at least potentially).

Where Beech focuses on artistic labor as the hinge, and the way in which the artist works, Brown focuses on art itself, Frankfurt School-style, combining Kant and Hegel to arrive at

---

4 Dave Beech, *Art and Value: Art's Economic Exceptionalism in Classical, Neoclassical and Marxist Economics* (Chicago: Haymarket, 2015), 9.
5 Ibid., 11.
6 Ibid., 28.

a definition of the artwork as that which has "purposiveness without external purpose." This lack of external purpose gives the artwork no purpose for the market, he argues, since unlike other commodities, there is no intention to exchange (though art is exchanged on the market, this is not what defines it as art). Its purpose and intentions are *internal,* which leads Brown to the conclusion that what defines an artwork is that it is *to be interpreted* (rather than exchanged): "To claim that something is a work of art is to claim that it is a self-legislating artifact, that its form is intelligible, but not by reference to any external end."[7] Interpretation — the process of making meaning from and with the work — involves not only figuring out whether a work succeeds, but what, in fact, it is trying to do.

Art's meaning has a social basis: what makes it "count," according to Brown, is how it intervenes in the institution of art: "Only by invoking the *institution* of art — a social machine that includes practices experienced as spontaneous, such as interpretation, as much as organized institutions such as museums, learned journals, academic departments — can the work of art assert its autonomy, which, again, holds sway only within its boundaries in the form of immanent purposiveness."[8] He invokes Bourdieu's concept of a "field of restricted production" to articulate the ways in which the social practices *around* art, which in his view center on meaning-making, can prevent the reduction of the work of art to the status of a simple commodity. This field of restricted production resists consumer sovereignty by creating a counter-public "of equals who are also competitors," who judge each other's works and "struggle over the significance of particular inventions," and is hailed by Brown as "the opposite of purchases on a market, which cannot provoke disagreement because […] no agreement is presupposed."[9]

---

7   Nicholas Brown, *Autonomy: The Social Ontology of Art under Capitalism* (Durham: Duke University Press, 2019), 39.
8   Ibid., 37.
9   Ibid., 18.

Brown admits that there is a tendency of art in the restricted field to gravitate toward formal concerns, working out problems specific to individual media: "What a restricted public of (for example) painters, critics of painting, and connoisseurs of painting share is nothing other than expertise in painting."[10] This, he notes, was the trajectory of modernism. But he sees other possibilities for the restricted field. For instance, meaning might reside "not in the formal reduction of an art to the problem of its medium but in a framing procedure, in the selection of a particular formal or thematic problem as central and the rewriting of the history of the medium or genre or even sociocultural aesthetic field as the history of that problem."[11] And while he doubles down on the artwork as the site of autonomy, and predictably inveighs against art practices that veer too close to politics, the attention he pays to the institution of art, and to the creation of meaning via that institution and the relation of individuals and society to it, suggests additional possibilities for the restricted field.[12]

If we think about art as an institution in the more expanded Castoriadian sense, as "a socially sanctioned, symbolic network in which a functional component and an imaginary component are combined,"[13] we can begin to fathom what those possibilities might be. As we have seen, Castoriadis also locates art's au-

---

10 Ibid.

11 Ibid., 25.

12 Whereas Brown perceives the public capable of engaging in this process as a limited one, the cognoscenti, Castoriadis argues that the publics in Western democracies from the eighteenth century through mid-twentieth century have been creative in their reception of culture, that is, they have been "caught up in the new meaning of the work [...] despite inertia, delays, resistances, and reaction" (Cornelius Castoriadis, "Culture in a Democratic Society," in *The Castoriadis Reader*, ed. and trans. David Ames Curtis [Oxford: Blackwell, 1997], 346). This is always a process of "re-creation" and never a matter of passive acceptance — and it's one way in which autonomy has gained ground in these societies, an essential part of the autonomy project as a whole.

13 Cornelius Castoriadis, *The Imaginary Institution of Society* (Cambridge: MIT Press, 1998), 132.

tonomy in its ability to produce meaning — in his case to give meaning to the products of the individual psyche:

> A phantasm remains a phantasm for a singular psyche, but artists, poets, musicians, and painters don't produce phantasms; they create works, *oeuvres*. What their imagination sires acquires a "real" — that is, social-historical-existence, and it does so by using an infinitude of means and elements — language, to begin with — that the artist could never have created "all by herself."[14]

This is especially true for modern art, Castoriadis argues, which "is able to exist only by questioning meaning as it [is] each time established and by creating other forms for it."[15] Thus, whether following from Marxist thought or psychoanalysis, art is characterized by its ability to make new meanings that escape heteronomy.

This suggests that, when it comes to the *art world*, which encompasses not only the institution of art as meaning-making process but also art institutions, there is a far greater possibility of redefining its core meanings. The institution of the "business enterprise," by contrast, rests solidly within the capitalist imaginary. As Castoriadis tells us:

> That institution conveys a signification, that set of arrangements and rules brings together large numbers of people, forces them to use specific tools and machines, controls their work and organizes it hierarchically, and its goal is its own unlimited self-aggrandizement. That institution and that signification are created by capitalism, and capitalism can only exist within and through this creation.[16]

---

14 Cornelius Castoriadis, "Primal Institution of Society and Second-Order Institutions," in *Figures of the Thinkable*, trans. Helen Arnold (Stanford: Stanford University Press, 2007), 99.
15 Castoriadis, "Culture in a Democratic Society," 345.
16 Castoriadis, "Primal Institution of Society and Second-Order Institutions," 100.

But while certainly "functionally" capitalist in our moment, art-as-institution, and art institutions, have another imaginary within their grasp.

And now for a little praxis: Let's take a look at recent events surrounding the call for the resignation of Whitney Museum board member Warren Kanders, a private defense manufacturer of tear gas canisters and smoke grenades used on protesters and asylum seekers around the world. Originated by Whitney staff in a collective letter to director Adam Weinberg in November 2018, the call was taken up first by the activist group Decolonize This Space, which organized nine weeks of protests at the museum, and then by over 120 academics, artists, and critics who ran an open letter on the Verso blog. W.A.G.E, an organization with the complicated mission of getting museums to pay wages to artists, initiated a call for an artist boycott of the Whitney Biennial in January, framing the act of solidarity they sought in terms of artists' using their "exceptional status as [workers] who can claim both the freedom to dissent and the right to be paid, to withhold their labor in solidarity with Whitney staff who cannot."[17]

Weinberg's public response to this "crisis of the Whitney" was to state: "Even as we are idealistic and missionary in our belief in artists, the Whitney is first and foremost a museum. It cannot right all the ills of an unjust world, nor is that its role."[18] The role of the museum, he quoted another museum director as saying, is "to make a safe space for unsafe ideas." In the safe space of the Whitney, Weinberg insisted, the "right to dissent" would be respected "as long as we can safeguard the art in our

---

17 Jasmine Weber, "W.A.G.E. Asks Artists to Demand Payment and Withhold Content from 2019 Whitney Biennial," *Hyperallergic,* January 23, 2019, https://hyperallergic.com/481246/w-a-g-e-asks-artists-to-demand-payment-and-withhold-content-from-2019-whitney-biennial.

18 Jasmine Weber, "Whitney Museum Director Pens Letter after Vice Chair's Relationship to Weapons Manufacturer Is Publicized," *Hyperallergic,* December 3, 2018, https://hyperallergic.com/474176/whitney-museum-director-pens-letter-after-vice-chairs-relationship-to-weapons-manufacturer-is-publicized.

care and the people in our midst." This, he proclaimed, "is the democracy of art."

Of course in this instance, the actions of a person in the Whitney's midst (a board vice chairman supplying tear gas to Border Patrol) were being challenged as inimical to the art and artists in the Whitney's "care" as well as other people — staff — also in the Whitney's midst. This was a move in the direction of the *radical* democracy of art. It couldn't, it's true, right all the ills of an unjust world, but nor was that its ambition. Its ambition was to dislodge the "reality" that art institutions *must* function like corporations, that their boards *must* resemble corporate boards, that their budgets *must* resemble corporate budgets, that they *must* grow or die (by 2000, the top 5 percent of U.S. visual art institutions controlled almost four-fifths of combined museum revenue, endowments, infrastructure, and donations[19]). That it didn't do so from within the already safe-for-capitalism space of the art world (à la institutional critique) but through solidarity among artists and museum workers and the activism of Decolonize This Space is what marked it as a genuinely unsafe (and therefore potentially transformative) idea.

"Calling out" individuals within art institutions is often viewed as a poor substitute for "effective" organizing, group psychology masquerading as political action. If all money is dirty money, goes the argument, then how is it anything other than reformism to refuse especially dirty money? First, it raises the possibility that money can be refused. And second, it creates the possibility of another institution, one that organizes itself rather than being organized by capitalist processes.

Interestingly, though one artist, Michael Rakowitz, did withdraw from the Biennial early on, it wasn't until Hannah Black, Ciarán Finlayson, and Tobi Haslett penned an open letter to participating artists in late July that artists withdrew from the

---

19 Melissa Smith, "MOMA's Budget Is About the Same Size as the Budget of 150 Museums in 1989 Combined," *Quartz*, May 24, 2014, https://qz.com/207299/momas-endowment-is-about-the-same-size-as-the-budget-of-150-museums-in-1989-combined/.

Biennial in any number. Brilliantly titled "The Teargas Biennial" (who wants their name associated with a Teargas Biennial?), the letter argued that their "withdrawal of work from the gallery [would disrupt] the actual circuits of valorization—not only of the work and its display in the prestigious museum, but of the museum and its stated interest in progressivism and socially committed art."[20] It called on artists to use their "extraordinary capacity to speak and be heard" to build on the work of Ferguson activists (who first identified the source of the tear gas bullets—also identified by activists in Palestine), students at Brown University (where Kanders was on the board), and again, the staff of the Whitney, in order to make Kanders vulnerable to protest. And it decried the "poverty of conditions" that convinces artists "they lack power in relation to the institutions their labor sustains," noting that "even the strategies of the historical avant-garde (oppositional independent salons, for instance) seem to have vanished from the realm of possibility, or no longer appear desirable, as institutions are treated like an omnipotent, irresistible force."[21]

Days after the letter was published, eight more artists withdrew from the Biennial, and Kanders himself quickly followed suit by resigning from the Whitney's board. In this way, the letter's logic was borne out—it was only once the *artists* turned against him that Kanders knew the gig was well and truly up, that the people "in his care" at the Whitney would no longer be complicit in and benefit from his acts of uncaring elsewhere. In doing so, these artists raised the possibility of radical institutional change, although the Whitney, with its forty-nine-million-dollar operating budget, is unlikely to voluntarily devolve into an oppositional independent salon anytime soon. But the prospect of coming untethered from its rich benefactors ("[some board members] worried that [Kanders's resignation]

---

20 Hannah Black, Ciarán Finlayson, and Tobi Haslett, "The Tear Gas Biennial," *Artforum*, July 17, 2019, https://www.artforum.com/slant/a-statement-from-hannah-black-ciaran-finlayson-and-tobi-haslett-on-warren-kanders-and-the-2019-whitney-biennial-80328.
21 Ibid.

would embolden protesters to demand the resignation of other board members"[22]) opened up possibilities for the institutions of art — and artists' role in challenging those institutions (including boards and biennials) — that had been foreclosed.

---

[22] Robin Pogrebin and Elizabeth A. Harris, "Warren Kanders Quits Whitney Board After Tear Gas Protests," *The New York Times,* July 25, 2019, https://www.nytimes.com/2019/07/25/arts/whitney-warren-kanders-resigns.html.

SEVENTEENTH LETTER

Autonomy, Meet Autonomy: On Art, Gentrification, and Refusal

Dear A,

Among other things, the Whitney protests underscored the power of open letters, didn't they? But a different set of protests, this one on the opposite coast, in a working-class Latinx neighborhood of Los Angeles called Boyle Heights, highlights other ways in which artists might practice a politics of autonomy in this moment.

The protests in Boyle Heights pinpointed the institution/enterprise of the gallery as an engine of real estate speculation, a scenario in which the presence of art world institutions (as opposed to artmaking, which exists everywhere), makes a neighborhood legible to the market as worthy of investment. As Martha Rosler describes, citing Sharon Zukin's analysis, in this process the intentions of individual artists matter little:

> The search among artists, creatives, and so forth, for a way of life that does not pave over older neighborhoods but infiltrates them with coffee shops, hipster bars, and clothing shops catering to their tastes, is a sad echo of the tourist paradigm centering on the indigenous authenticity of the place they have colonized. The authenticity of these urban neigh-

borhoods, with their largely working-class populations, is characterized not by bars and bodegas so much as by what the press calls grit, signifying the lack of bourgeois polish. [...] The arrival in numbers of artists, hipsters, and those who follow — no surprise here! — brings about the eradication of this initial appeal. And, as detailed in *Loft Living,* the artists and hipsters are in due course driven out by wealthier folk, by the abundant vacant lofts converted to luxury dwellings or the new construction in the evacuated manufacturing zones. Unfortunately, many artists who see themselves evicted in this process fail to see, or persist in ignoring, the role that artists have played in occupying these formerly "alien" precincts.[1]

Much of what Rosler describes above played out in Boyle Heights, similarly to other neighborhoods on LA's Eastside — until it didn't. In 2016, Boyle Heights activists adopted a militant strategy of insisting that all twelve galleries and art spaces that had opened in the neighborhood in the previous decade close themselves down, a gesture that stripped away the benign face of gentrification, its seeming organicism to those carrying it out on the street-by-street, building-by-building level (as opposed to the planners and developers), and reframed the art world as allied with global capitalism and hypergentrification. The blockade extended even to Self-Help Graphics, a gallery, workshop, and community space that had been in operation in the neighborhood for more than forty years, because of the organization's more recent ties to developers and art world donors. The call for Self-Help to leave Boyle Heights along with the galleries failed to gain traction ultimately, arguably because of this history, but it exerted pressure on the organization to reaffirm its original mission.

---

1   Martha Rosler, "Culture Class: Art, Creativity, Urbanism, Part II," *e-flux* 23 (March, 2011), https://www.e-flux.com/journal/23/67813/culture-class-art-creativity-urbanism-part-ii/.

The stories of two other spaces that were eventually forced out of the neighborhood have much to tell us. The first of these was a gallery called PSSST, which moved into Boyle Heights in 2016 with the mission of "artists supporting artists [...] by valuing process over product and community over singular success." Helmed by two recent art school grads, PSSST planned to work primarily with underrepresented artists. Little did they know, apparently, that the gallery had set up shop in a neighborhood with a profound and hard-won commitment to political autonomy, which immediately brought their intentions under intense scrutiny.

As Carribean Fragoza details, for twenty years prior to the arrive of PSSST, Boyle Heights residents had been organizing against racism, gang violence, drug epidemics, and poverty.[2] Union de Vecinos, a tenants rights organization, had been active in the neighborhood ever since the demolition of the Pico-Aliso public housing projects in the late nineties, while in the early nineties, a group of mothers, parishioners of Delores Mission Church, teamed up with Father Gregory Boyle to confront gang violence with "love walks" through the neighborhood, offering food and conversation to gang members engaged in nightly battles. Naming themselves the Comite Pro Paz En El Barrio, they listened to the young men's stories of police brutality and responded by integrating a "cop watch" component into their mission, in place of the "neighborhood watch" model to which they had previously subscribed.[3]

Boyle Heights in 2016 was thus not just an abandoned industrial zone with huge empty warehouses and cold storage units and cheap rents, it was also a community where the people who had lost their jobs in those facilities had organized to keep their rents affordable and their lives livable. Nor was PSSST

---

[2] Carribean Fragoza, "Art and Complicity: How the Fight Against Gentrification in Boyle Heights Questions the Role of Artists," *KCET*, July 20, 2016, https://www.kcet.org/shows/artbound/boyle-heights-gentrification-art-galleries-pssst.

[3] William Ury, "Gang Warfare: Mothers as Thirdsiders," *The Third Side*, https://thirdside.williamury.com/mothers-as-thirdsiders/.

itself merely a scrappy storefront art space helmed by a couple of young artists striking out on their own. It was supported with a free twenty-year lease from an anonymous donor who'd spent two million dollars to acquire and renovate the building. There were other forces afoot in the neighborhood as well: a development corporation, the Fifteen Group, which planned to demolish 1,175 rent-controlled units and build 4,150 new market rate units, and the newly formed Boyle Heights Alliance Against Art-Washing and Displacement (BHAAAD), which included community organizations Defend Boyle Heights, Union de Vecinos, and the Comite Pro Paz, as well as the long-lasting artivist collective Ultra Red.

Throughout 2016, BHAAAD protesters targeted a swathe of recently opened Boyle Heights art spaces in addition to PSSST, including the United Talent Agency Artist Space, Venus Over Los Angeles, MaRS, and 356 Mission. They issued mock eviction notices, picketed openings, graffitied the spaces' external walls with slogans such as NO MORE WHITE ART and spattered them with shit. Similar to PSSST, 356 Mission, an artist-run space with ties to the commercial art world (founded by painter Laura Owens and her gallerist Gavin Brown), became a flashpoint in this conflict over art's role in gentrification processes — much more so than the other, unabashedly commercial galleries that were also targeted. To many in the LA art world, this targeting was baffling — this was a space, after all, that wasn't operating according to the profit motive. 356 Mission described itself on its website as "a collaborative project that prioritizes cultural and arts programming that is open and available to everyone[, …] not a business geared toward financial gain." Surely they had more in common with BHAAAD than with the galleries?

Things came to a head when 356 Mission hosted the inaugural meeting of a group called the Artists Political Action Committee, formed in February 2017 in response to Trump's election.[4] BHAAAD protesters picketed the meeting and urged

---

4   Catherine G. Wagley, "Good-Bye to All That: Boyle Heights, Hotbed of Gentrification Protests, Sees Galleries Depart," *ARTnews,* June 8, 2018,

artists not to enter the building. As Travis Diehl observes: "The solidarity art-worlders felt — or sought — after Trump's election did not erase the hard line drawn by BHAAAD and its affiliates between those art venues gentrifying Boyle Heights, unwittingly or otherwise, and those fighting to preserve it in its present state. Artists who showed up for the APAN meeting had to choose between crossing the picket line or turning back."[5] Nizan Shaked, describing her own experience of the picket line, recounts a conversation she had with a protester before she did turn back: "'I have no place in that world,' a protester told me," to which Shaked responded, "'But most of those people inside do not either.' […] 'The vast majority live under precarious conditions — they have no job, living, studio or health care security.'" Shaked then asks of the reader: "Why does this art world crowd support a system in which only a handful of them will end up making a living by selling their art or landing a tenured job? If we really mean to come together in solidarity, how can we not take the protesters' side?"[6]

What it means to come together in solidarity — that is, to position the autonomy of art and art institutions in alignment with, rather than as opposed to, autonomous politics — was the central question at the heart of the conflict in Boyle Heights. In a statement published in *Artforum* in November 2017, Owens gave her perspective on the APAN event and picket:

> In February of 2017 for the first time a few protestors came to an event we hosted, falsely implying that the space is linked to developers and is directly responsible for the displacement of low income residents. I respect people's right to protest in a

---

http://www.artnews.com/2018/06/08/good-bye-boyle-heights-hotbed-gentrification-protests-sees-galleries-depart/.

5 Travis Diehl, "Op-ed: An Ultra-red Line," *X-tra Online,* October 12, 2017, https://www.x-traonline.org/online/travis-diehl-op-ed-an-ultra-red-line/.

6 Nizan Shaked, "How to Draw a (Picket) Line: Activists Protest Event at Boyle Heights Gallery," *Hyperallergic,* February 14, 2017, https://hyperallergic.com/358652/how-to-draw-a-picket-line-activists-protest-event-at-boyle-heights-gallery/.

safe and non-violent manner and to have their voices heard. While we disagreed with their rhetoric and accusations, we shared the goal to create a more just housing market. The relationship between art and gentrification is an urgent issue for the art community to discuss and should be further explored thoughtfully and respectfully between artists, civic leaders, and most importantly the residents of the neighborhood.[7]

In her statement, Owens emphasizes shared goals, support for dissent, and a need for discussion, while noting ruefully that protesters refused to engage in a dialogue and at their only face-to-face meeting rejected 356's ideas for collaboration, "such as working together on community land buy backs, campaigning for specific policy changes, providing laundromat services and sponsoring workshops for kids."[8] Noting that the only idea the protesters themselves presented in that meeting was for 356 to dissolve and hand over the keys to the building to them "for unspecified purposes," Owens concluded that this was a demand that wouldn't in fact slow development and instead offered up another point of commonality between the inhabitants of Boyle Heights and the staff and community of 356 Mission: a belief that "art and basic needs shouldn't be in conflict in a thriving society."[9]

But it soon became clear that the purpose of the protests was to refuse points of commonality and to underscore schisms, driving home a point of difference: that the art world is in lockstep with a system that allows only parts of society to thrive, and to thrive off the immiseration of others. As the women of Pico Aliso expressed in an open letter to Owens: "It was many years with fear throwing ourselves to the floor because of the bullets, asking the police to respect us and looking for programs

---

7 "Laura Owens Responds to Protests of 356 S. Mission Rd.," *Artforum International,* November 14, 2017, https://www.artforum.com/news/laura-owens-responds-to-protests-of-356-s-mission-rd-72259.
8 Ibid.
9 Ibid.

and improvements for our community. [...] Now that our community has improved, artists arrive with their galleries and their coffee shops, close our businesses, raise our rents."[10]

What the protests were after was something more seismic than dialogue, which is the acknowledgment of differences in the experience of class and race — and the art world's role in perpetuating them — that cannot be resolved through liberal democratic channels. This wasn't a naïve stance, a regrettable misreading of the situation, "non-artworlders" mistaking friendly artists for dastardly developers; it was a politics and a set of tactics. Some of those politics and tactics — particularly the Maoist ones — were authoritarian, leveraging a heteronomy that arguably blocked a meaningful outcome of the conflict, but they also injected strategic militancy into the residents' long history of organizing for collective control over the neighborhood. "The only way we are heard is when you say no," said Leonardo Vilchis of Union de Vecinos. "And that's terrifying because you're a jerk who says no. But we have had more negotiations now since we've said no than if we had said yes."[11]

It's tempting to try to imagine what 356 Mission might have done differently with the benefit of hindsight. The speed of gentrification and hypergentrification today provides only a short window of time in which art spaces in similar circumstances might try to do anything other than serve as "foot soldiers of displacement," as Magally Miranda and Kyle Lane-McKinley frame their role, noting the cognitive dissonance between the "economic analysis of effects of artwashing and the stated intentions of such groups toward inclusivity, multiculturalism and

---

10 Nizan Shaked, "Why I Am Resigning from X-TRA Contemporary Art Quarterly and the Problem with 356 Mission's Politics," *Hyperallergic*, April 27, 2018, https://hyperallergic.com/440234/x-tra-contemporary-art-quarterly-356-mission-boyle-heights/.

11 Carolina A. Miranda, "'Out! Boyle Heights Activists Say White Art Elites Are Ruining the Neighborhood ... But It's Complicated," *Los Angeles Times*, October 14, 2016, https://www.latimes.com/entertainment/arts/miranda/la-et-cam-art-gentrification-boyle-heights-20161014-snap-story.html.

even radicality."¹² For me, this cognitive dissonance manifested in a curious way. In conversations with artist and activists about the blockade, I found myself referring to 356 as 365 — a simple transposition but perhaps not without significance, 365 being the Whole Foods subsidiary designed to pitch cheaper products to younger consumers, the up-and-coming gentrifying class. Clearly, my brain was gnawing on the question: How could 356 not become 365? Was it already 365? Or was still there enough of a difference for something else to happen there?

This was the question posed by Tracy Jeanne Rosenthal, an art writer and member of the LA Tenants Union, in an open letter responding to Owens:

> What would it be like to enter a dialogue [with the protesters] without demanding to be left intact? I think they call those kinds of dialogues negotiations. I'm sure we all know some negotiating tactics, from jobs, from organizing, or even from the movies. They say leave. You could say, we'll give you half. In this case, I don't know what that half would be. Would it come in resources? In square feet? Nor is it my place to say whether it should be accepted. But I admit I am naive enough to think you would have made an offer.¹³

By emphasizing "negotiations" as opposed to "dialogue," the protesters — and Rosenthal here — were proposing something similar to the "land back" concept deployed by indigenous groups historically and today, which as Eve Tuck and K. Wayne Yang argue, eschews decolonization as metaphor for decolonization as process: "Though the details are not fixed or agreed

---

12 Magally Miranda and Kyle Lane-McKinley, "Artwashing, or, Between Social Practice and Social Reproduction," *A Blade of Grass,* February 1, 2017, http://www.abladeofgrass.org/fertile-ground/artwashing-social-practice-social-reproduction/.

13 Tracy Jeanne Rosenthal, "Contributor Tracy Jeanne Rosenthal Responds to Laura Owens," *Daily Gentrifier,* November 27, 2017, https://thedailygentrifier.com/news/2017/11/27/tracy-rosenthal-responds-to-laura-owens-la-artwashing (site discontinued).

upon, […] decolonization in the settler colonial context must involve the repatriation of land simultaneous to the recognition of how land and relations to land have always already been differently understood and enacted; that is, all of the land, and not just symbolically."[14] This, they note, is why "decolonization is necessarily unsettling."[15] And of course, there was another "land back" process immanent in the demands for current Boyle Heights residents to gain full or partial control over 356 Mission: the restoration of that property and all of Boyle Heights to the Tongva people.

But Rosenthal's proposal raises another question: Why did she *think* Owens would have made an offer that did not leave her own vision for 356 intact (or that Gavin Brown or his insurers would allow it, for that matter)? That is to say, why did Rosenthal's expectations for an artist-run space include this mutability of form, this lack of proprietariness, this communeism or intercommunalism (and again, why did the protesters themselves target this artist-run space versus the commercial galleries)? As we've seen, there's a notion of the autonomy of art and the artist that integrates easily into capitalist processes, the one based on the assumption, as Miranda and Lane-Mckinley describe it, that the artist-as-individual "is accountable only to him or her self," which in the context of neoliberal capitalism "too often results, de facto, in their being accountable only to the entrepreneurial endeavors of powerful institutions."[16] But there's also the other notion of autonomy, which raises the expectation that artists' ability to create new forms would also extend to new forms of collectivity — that autonomization can function as a counterpower to capitalist organizing processes. As we've seen, this potential is explicitly articulated in relational art, but it's also latent in art's materialism — surely those who can continually find new meanings for materials and objects know on some

---

14 Eve Tuck and K.Wayne Yang, "Decolonization Is Not a Metaphor," *Decolonization: Indigeneity, Education and Society* 1, no. 1 (2012): 7.

15 Ibid., 7.

16 Miranda and Lane-McKinley, "Artwashing, or, Between Social Practice and Social Reproduction."

profound level that society, too, can be made anew. Autonomy is not just a politics for relational art, but for all art.

Another dynamic at play in the struggle over 356 Mission (symbolic or otherwise), was the fact that the space itself was largely devoted to painting (Owens is a painter and Gavin Brown originally opened the space to show a series of her especially large paintings; much of the art exhibited there by others was painting). As a "restricted public," its community was largely a formalist one, and not engaged in a critique of the art world's relation to capital (nor its race or gender politics for that matter). Rather, it conformed to art's assigned role as capitalism's internal, "unemphatic other," as Nicholas Brown describes it, taking on the function of what Marcuse calls "affirmative culture," which is to provide a modicum of freedom under generally exploitative conditions. So perhaps it's not surprising that 356 itself functioned as an unemphatic other to the galleries surrounding it, and to the gallery system as a whole, rather than emphatically coming down on the side of an autonomous politics that challenged capitalist processes of organization in the art world and beyond. Not surprising, but not inevitable.

One of the lessons delivered by BHAAAD's organizing in Boyle Heights is that art's alignment with capital can't just be wished away — it takes effort to find our way to another imaginary. This is not a matter of artists *relinquishing* their claim to autonomy but rather of developing it *further,* in ways that acknowledge the social politicity of art. Certainly art's emplacement, including the supposedly neutral codes of art spaces, must be reexamined (Brian O'Dougherty's 1976 description of "pictures laid out in a row like expensive bungalows" comes to mind).[17] But autonomy also tells us things can always be different next time. Rosenthal mourns the absence of a "reckoning" in the case of 356 (which quietly closed its doors in fall of 2018), and adds, "I think a lot

---

17 Brian O'Dougherty, *Inside the White Cube: The Ideology of the Gallery Space* (Santa Monica: Lapis Press, 1976), 29. See also Travis Diehl, "White-Wall White," *East of Borneo,* October 12, 2017, https://eastofborneo.org/articles/white-wall-white/.

of us want to make art or be around it without being a force for gentrification. I wonder what prevents us from believing we have enough power to make that real."[18] The answer is *everything* and *nothing*.

---

[18] Rosenthal, "Contributor Tracy Jeanne Rosenthal Responds to Laura Owens."

EIGHTEENTH LETTER

On Educating for Autonomy and the Early Years of CalArts

Dear A,

I think it has become clear that the question of how to get from here to there—how to begin to *move*—is one that occupies all manifestations of the autonomy project. Castoriadis viewed an emancipatory education as one way to move out of the impasse at the heart of his own formulation of autonomy, which is that only autonomous collectivities can socialize individuals capable of accessing the radical imagination, but autonomous individuals must already exist in order to create those autonomous collectivities.

A society that was radically democratic would have what he calls a "non-mutilating" education, or *paideia,* that develops the autonomy of both individual and collective by encouraging self-reflection in *both* registers. But on the way to *paideia* (and a radically democratic society where order-givers and order-takers are a thing of the past), we must have an education that somehow enables us to break with our socialization and envision other forms of being and being together. Emancipatory education, like art (and also, for Castoriadis, psychoanalysis), serves the function of connecting the "reflective subject (of will and thought) and [their] Unconscious—that is, [their] radical imagination."¹ This makes of the thinking subject a creative one as well, freeing their capacity "to make and do things, to form an open project for [their] life and to work with that project."² Such an education would also — in its closest instantiation to *paideia* — need to foreground the mutability of the pedagogical situation. This, too, must not only be questioned but remade.

I think a lot about the possibilities for emancipatory education, because I teach in a place where what it means to teach and what it means to learn is under continuous interrogation. I think this is because it's an art school, but also because it's a particular kind of art school, founded at a particular time, and oriented toward a particular kind of art. CalArts formed fifty years ago with an apparent schism at its core. Dreamed up by Walt Disney, progenitor of world entertainment capitalism, it culled its first faculty from the ranks of the New York avant-garde.³ What's more, it came to life at a time when the conventions of schooling were under enormous pressure, both from theorists of critical pedagogy such as Paolo Freire and Ivan Illich, whose most celebrated books, *Pedagogy of the Oppressed and Deschooling Society* respectively, were published in the same cultural moment, and from the student movement lighting up college campuses around the country with demands for democratization and self-determination.

In *Pedagogy of the Oppressed,* Freire critiques the dominant "banking" model of learning for treating education as the act of depositing knowledge into students, advocating instead for a "problem-solving" model that fosters "acts of cognition" rather

---

1   Ingerid Straume, "Paidea," in *Cornelius Castoriadis: Key Concepts,* ed. Suzi Adams (London: Bloomsbury, 2014), 151.
2   Cornelius Castoriadis, "Psychoanalysis and Politics," in *World in Fragments: Writings on Politics, Society, Psychoanalysis, and the Imagination,* ed. and trans. David Ames Curtis (Stanford: Stanford University Press, 1997), 132.
3   Portions of this letter having to do with CalArts previously appeared in my essay "Teaching (Which Is Not Teaching) Art (Which Is Not Art)," in *Where Art Might Happen: The Early Years of Calarts,* eds. Philipp Kaiser and Christina Vegh (Munich: Prestel Publishing, 2021), 155–68.

than "transferrals of information."[4] He encourages students and teachers to enter into dialogue in order to problem solve together, resulting in new subject positions: "The teacher is no longer merely the-one-who-teaches, but one who is himself taught in dialogue with the student, who in turn while being taught also teaches."[5] Illich, meanwhile, seeks to do away with curriculum altogether, arguing that "all over the world the school has an anti-educational effect on society."[6] School merely produces the demand for schooling, he maintains, when in fact "learning is the human activity which least needs manipulation by others. Most learning is not the result of instruction. It is rather the result of unhampered participation in a meaningful setting."[7] To arrive at a different model for education we must question "the very idea of publicly prescribed learning, rather than the methods used in its enforcement."[8]

Elements of these critiques were evident in CalArts's early promotional literature — including statements by Disney himself, whose own education was unconventional (he took night classes in high school at the Art Institute of Chicago, and left school at age sixteen) — which either explicitly redefined the notion of "school" or steered clear of the word altogether. The "Concept" statement that appeared in the first CalArts admissions bulletin reads in part: "California Institute of the Arts is more than a professional school; it is a community with a new concept. Our students will be accepted as artists. We assume they have come to develop the talents they bring. They are treated accordingly and are encouraged in the independence that this implies."[9] The bulletin emphasizes CalArts' function as a

---

4   Paolo Freire, *Pedagogy of the Oppressed*, trans. Myra Bergman Ramos (London: Bloomsbury Academic, 2000), 72.
5   Ibid., 80.
6   Ivan Illich, *Deschooling Society* (London: Marion Boyars, 1971), 8.
7   Ibid., 39.
8   Ibid., 65.
9   See *Arts in Society* 7, no. 3, special issue: "California Institute of the Arts: Prologue to a Community," eds. Sheila de Bretteville, Barry Hyams, and Marianne Partridge (Fall–Winter 1970): 16, https://digicoll.library.wisc.edu/cgi-bin/Arts/Arts-idx?id=Arts.ArtsSocv07i3.

"laboratory" or "performance center" and valorizes experience over structure, equality over hierarchy: "The training program is thought of as a context of experience in which solutions to real problems can be discovered. [...] Students and faculty perform as collaborators."[10] As Judith Adler notes in her definitive 1979 ethnography of CalArts, *Artists in Offices,* "Reference to the new organization as an *institute* (with its connotations of scientific and scholarly prestige) and as a *community* implicitly distinguished CalArts from other schools where artists *teach* students."[11] Central to this formation of a community of artists was the parallel idea of a community of art *forms,* embraced both by Disney (think *Fantasia*) and many of the faculty, who were themselves experimenting with medium and genre crossings.

Planning for the school took the form not of laying out conventional pedagogical structures but of amassing a "'center of energy' created by the 'chemistry' of bringing together all the 'right people.'"[12] To begin with, Disney charged none other than H.R. Haldeman (soon to become Richard Nixon's chief of staff but at that time an advertising exec and the first chair of the CalArts Board of Trustees) with the mission of finding the best practitioners in their fields to serve as the institute's first administrators.[13] The new deans, in their turn, focused on recruiting

---

10 *CalArts Admissions Bulletin 1969–1970,* Series 12.1, CalArts Publications 1963–87, CalArts Archive, California Institute of the Arts, Valencia, California.

11 Judith Adler, *Artists in Offices: An Ethnography of an Academic Art Scene* (New York: Routledge, 2017), 102.

12 Ibid.

13 President Robert Corrigan had been dean of NYU's School of the Performing Arts and a drama scholar; Provost and Theater Dean Herbert Blau had been director of the Repertory Theater at Lincoln Center; Paul Brach (Dean of Art), chair of the art department at UC San Diego; Mel Powell (Dean of Music), chair of the music department at Yale; Maurice Stein (Dean of Critical Studies), chair of the sociology department at Brandeis; Alexander MacKendrick (Dean of Film), Hollywood film director; and Richard E. Farson (Dean of Design), director of the Western Behavioral Sciences Training Institute.

faculty above all else. As Mel Powell, Dean of the Music School, insisted in an early planning meeting: "We must know by now that curricula, or especially descriptions of curricula, are almost always humbug. What counts is the people involved."[14] A similar approach was taken to fostering interdisciplinarity; as Provost Herbert Blau recalled:

> In order to assure ourselves that the barriers between the arts would indeed be broken down, [...] we looked especially for people who because of the nature of their own work required such an environment; so that we were not simply talking about interdisciplinary work in the arts but we were dealing with people who had an internal disposition toward this view of reality.[15]

In this way, the forms of pedagogy practiced at the new institute took their shape from the artists and forms of art being made there, leading in turn to the development of new art forms. The "Post-Studio Art" class, for instance, was designed by John Baldessari, who was initially hired onto the faculty as a painter, despite the fact that he had famously burned all of his paintings in 1968. Given total latitude to decide what and how he wanted to teach, Baldessari expressed a desire to work with "students who don't paint or do sculpture or any other activity by hand."[16] He then devoted himself to creating the right environment for these students, providing primarily equipment (super-8 cameras, video cameras, still cameras); exposure to the exciting roster of New York and European conceptual artists he brought to campus as visitors; and exhibition catalogues. "If you had enough good artists around from all over," he reasoned, "the students would come and they would teach each other."[17]

---

14 Quoted in Adler, *Artists in Offices*, 102.
15 Herbert Blau, "Disney's Dough Takes Flight," March 7, 1970, Berkeley, CA, KPFA radio broadcast.
16 John Baldessari, "Reflections," in *Jack Goldstein and the CalArts Mafia*, ed. Richard Herz (Ojai: Minneola Press, 2003), 74.
17 Ibid., 63.

Baldessari deliberately sought to blur the boundaries between art making and teaching, noting: "The reason I got into teaching was that it was the closest thing to art I could be doing to make a living; it wasn't art, and it wasn't actually teaching. [...] I was going at my class much like I would do art, which was basically trying to be as formed as possible but open to chance.[18] It was this third space between form and chance that for Baldessari created the ideal conditions for art to happen, and like many other CalArts faculty of the period, he literalized that notion by moving students out of the pedagogical space of the institute and into the landscape of Southern California: "One of my tricks was that we'd have a map up on the wall, and somebody would just throw a dart at the map, and we would go there that day. [...] Try to do art around where we were." Unconstrained by a conventional pedagogical space — physical or ideological — but moving freely in and out of the building and in and out of the structures of knowledge and experience traditionally associated with schools, teachers and students alike were able to develop forms of teaching-that-is-not-teaching and art-that-is-not-art (i.e., that broke with the conventions of art).

This was certainly true of the Feminist Art Program, which began in the institute's second year and famously took shape in and through an off-campus space known as Womanhouse. Over the course of a month, faculty and students transformed a condemned mansion in Hollywood into a giant installation commenting on the strictures of domesticity and femininity, with a progression of breast sculptures turning gradually to fried eggs on the kitchen wall, a massive collection of used tampons in the bathroom, and a mannequin trapped in the linen closet. As Arlene Raven observes: "Repairing and structuring the house as an independent exhibition space as well as a work of art in itself was a vital element in a course of study and work designed to build

---

18 Christopher Knight, "A Situation Where Art Might Happen: John Baldessari on CalArts," *East of Borneo*, November 19, 2011, https://eastofborneo.org/articles/a-situation-where-art-might-happen-john-baldessari-on-calarts/.

students' skills and teach them to work cooperatively. [...] [T]he nature of the work ranged from cleaning to construction, labor that crossed not only class and gender lines, but that was outside of the scope of 'art.'"[19] Womanhouse was open to the public as an exhibition/performance space for the month of February 1972, after which the Feminist Art Program (FAP), helmed by Judy Chicago and Miriam Schapiro, moved into a large, fully equipped studio on campus. There, the twenty-five women students enrolled in the program, and many others who were not, engaged in a participatory art pedagogy informed by feminist principles, of which Womanhouse was a prime example.

Combining consciousness-raising sessions that grappled with taboo subjects like rape, domestic abuse, sexual harassment, and mother/daughter relationships, with research into women's issues and the history of women artists, Chicago and Shapiro's program provided an experience of individual and collective autonomy that went far beyond the institution of art. As Faith Wilding, a graduate of the program, observes:

> We were connected to a much larger enterprise than trying to advance our artistic careers, or to make art for art's sake. It was precisely our commitment to the activist politics of women's liberation, to a burgeoning theory and practice of feminism, and to a larger conversation about community, collectivity and radical history, which has given me lasting connections to people, and a continuing sense of being part of a cultural and political resistance, however fragmentary the expression of this may be in my life today.[20]

FAP's emplacement at CalArts led to a cross-pollination with conceptual art practices (particularly Fluxus and Kaprow) that

---

19 Arlene Raven, "Womanhouse," in *The Power of Feminist Art*, eds. Judith Brodsky, Norma Broude, and Mary Garraude (New York: Harry Abrams, 1994), 50.
20 Faith Wilding, "Written in the Sand: Letter to (Young) Women Artist and Art Historians," in *re:tracing the feminist art program*, ed. Ulrike Muller, http://www.encore.at/retracing/index2.html.

was central to the development of a new form: feminist performance art, which troubled both emerging feminist art conventions and conceptual art ones. As Lacy recalls: "Because he was working so closely with many of us feminists, Allan [Kaprow's] work gave us a foundation for the move into "life" that we were looking for in a political sense. He gave us a rationale for it. Obviously Judy is herself a strong visual formalist, but her teaching was for expression, expression, expression, whereas Allan's teaching methodology was cool, discursive, anything was possible, everything was interesting to discuss. [...] He also was the first person to introduce me to nontheatrical performance."[21]

Though not as well documented as Post Studio and FAP, Fluxus was another important locus of experimental teaching and learning at the early institute. Fluxus artists populated — and collaborated across — various schools at the outset: Alison Knowles, Peter Van Riper, and Kaprow in the School of Art; Dick Higgins in the School of Design; Emmett Williams in the School of Critical Studies; James Tenney in Music; and Nam Jun Paik in Film. The institute's eschewal of grades, its flexible timetable to graduation, and its highly improvisatory weekly schedule created fertile conditions for Fluxus pedagogy, which, as Hannah Higgins has noted, emphasized not only "experiential learning, but also interdisciplinary exploration, self-directed study, collective work, and the nonhierarchical exchange of ideas."[22]

Alternative uses of space by Fluxus-related artists, including scripted activities organized by Kaprow's Advanced Happenings class, played a key role in shaping — or de-forming — the early CalArts environment. One of the more prominent of these projects involved a pair of sinuous biomorphic sculptures entitled *House of Dust*, which Alison Knowles repurposed for the new

---

21 Moira Roth, "Suzanne Lacy on the Feminist Art Program at Fresno and Calarts," *East of Borneo*, December 15, 2011, https://eastofborneo.org/articles/suzanne-lacy-on-the-feminist-program-at-fresno-state-and-calarts.
22 Hannah Higgins, *Fluxus Experience* (Berkeley: University of California Press, 2002), 189.

campus upon its opening in 1969.²³ "I had these huge sculptures coming in on a flatbed truck that had to be activated," she recalls, "and I wasn't going to have them just sit on the land. They were weird-looking things but they were important because the building itself was so unfortunate — I felt you might as well put an apartment house there. So I would have my classes and my meetings out at the *House of Dust* and we had a rail to run sound lines out there so we could do readings and we had quite a number of food events."²⁴

In the context of the fledgling institute, Knowles's social sculpture raised all kinds of questions: What is it to make a house your school, your school a house? How is a schoolhouse different from a school building? How might a Fluxus house, a Fluxus school be different? How does the intimacy of the house counterpose the bureaucracy of the educational institution? How does it reframe the practice of the everyday, combining intellectual and bodily life? How might it, similarly to Womanhouse, destabilize gender role expectations, transforming the meaning of "housework"? Who does it bring together who might not come together otherwise? What can we learn there that we cannot learn elsewhere?

By now you'll have noticed a general tendency in the practices of both art and teaching I describe here: that old avant-garde pipe dream, the merging of art and life. As Peter Burger famously argues, the avant-garde has been characterized throughout its history by the attempt to direct the aesthetic experience toward the practical, paradoxically stripping it of its otherness: "What most strongly conflicts with the means-ends rationality of bour-

---

23 The "House of Dust" was the material embodiment of one quatrain of her and Tenney's famous computerized poem by the same name: "a House of Dust on open ground lit by natural light, inhabited by friends and enemies."

24 Janet Sarbanes, "A School Based on What Artists Wanted to Do: Alison Knowles on CalArts," *East of Borneo,* August 7, 2012, https://eastofborneo.org/articles/a-school-based-on-what-artists-wanted-to-do-alison-knowles-on-calarts/.

geois society, [Art], is to become life's organizing principle."[25] Though the avant-garde failed in its stated aim of dissolving art into life, Burger argues, it succeeded in revealing the function of art in bourgeois society, because the attack on its autonomy makes art visible as an institution that determines both "the productive and distributive apparatus and also [...] the ideas about art that prevail at a given time and that determine the reception of works."[26]

What is missing from this by now canonical analysis is an acknowledgment that the avant-garde assault on the autonomy of art is a movement from *within* pushing out. It's not a heteronomy, as Burger depicts it, but a further autonomization of the institution of art, which seeks to make art's autonomy matter *more,* opening up the social politicity of art practices to refashioning by both formal and non-formal means. As we've seen, this opening can be called forth by political autonomies that bring the radical imaginary once more into view; it can also occur through a formalization of affect that mounts its own resistance to heteronomy, a b(e)aring of feeling. It can happen in many ways, none of which suggests a failure to understand the way art works — that failure belongs to the critical apparatus.

In the case of CalArts, art's autonomy intersected with the autonomy of the "art school" in meaningful ways, particularly since Corrigan and Blau "tried to reflect in the conception of the Institute — in its structure — the structure of the arts themselves," maintaining that the time had come for "a place to exist which draws its principles of behavior from the work it is meant to develop and encourage as it goes along."[27] This essentially poietic guiding principle, preserved, for instance, in the school deans' dual role as practicing artists and administrators, means that the institute has always mounted a dual challenge to the institution of art and the institution of school. It has a functional

---

25 Peter Burger, *Theory of the Avant-Garde* (Minneapolis: University of Minnesota Press, 1984), 22.

26 Ibid.

27 Blau, "Disney's Dough Takes Flight."

component, to be sure, but combined with an imaginary component that prevents it from ever taking a final form.[28]

As "Disney's School," CalArts has also had continually to define itself as something other than that most paradigmatic of capitalist institutions: the corporation. In this respect, institute faculty may have gotten the jump on their peers at other institutions of higher learning in coming to understand that autonomy must be fought for. Battles they lost: in 1970, Marcuse would have been hired by the School of Critical Studies (where I teach) were it not for the redbaiting protestations of the board, then populated largely by Disney corporation executives, who also fired Corrigan and Blau at the end of their second year. The war they won, by defining their teaching as an open-ended creative practice, not a skills delivery service: total autonomy in the classroom. Called forth by autonomous political movements, the autonomy of art in turn called forth an autonomous education — this is how autonomies reinforce each other across spheres and institutions, this is how autonomy grows.[29] That said, CalArts today saddles its students with massive debt, like many other private institutions and more and more public institutions in the U.S. and increasingly elsewhere. Some wars are world wars.

Indeed, as higher education, like art institutions, becomes more and more organized by neoliberal capitalist processes, it's

---

28 I always enjoy the moment when a younger colleague is asked, what do you teach at CalArts? and they preface their answer with a question, "What *do* I teach?" I was that younger colleague once, truly unmoored from anything I had been trained for as an English PhD, struggling to understand what I was expected to do in this place where the curriculum was continually being rethought and remade. What was my job? While Adler sees the word "Institute" in the school's name as a bid for prestige, over the years I've come to think of it more as an exhortation — INSTITUTE!

29 Note Patrisse Cullors's recent activities: earning an MFA in Social Practice in 2019 (from a USC program headed by Suzanne Lacy), directing an online MFA in Social Practice program at Prescott College and cofounding the Crenshaw Dairy Mart, a new art space in Los Angeles, while continuing to work against local prison initiatives with Dignity & Power Now, an organization she founded.

difficult to imagine growing the autonomy project on college campuses in any real way without serious and sustained counter-organizing against student debt, instrumentalized learning, administrative heteronomy, the adjunctification of professors, the precarity of staff and the policing of campuses. This is in fact the *only* way to revive education's investment in autonomy in any radical sense. As Takis Fotopoulos argues, "Just as [Castoradis's] paideia is only feasible within the framework of a genuine democracy, an emancipatory education is inconceivable outside a democratic movement fighting for such a society."[30] As part of this movement, faculty and students can exercise the autonomy we still retain and work to grow it, individually and collectively, in and beyond our institutions. In every classroom, there's a social sculpture underway, constructed out of ideas, relationships, and the desire to be free. This is where — and how — the struggle begins.

---

30 Takis Fotopoulos, "From (Mis)education to *Paideia*," *International Journal of Inclusive Democracy* 2, no. 1 (September 2005), https://www.inclusivedemocracy.org/journal/vol2/vol2_no1_miseducation_paideia_takis.htm.

LAST LETTER

Not an End But a Beginning

Dear A,

When I first conceived of this book, I thought to model it on Friedrich Schiller's *On the Aesthetic Education of Man in A Series of Letters,* a main argument of which—that art can help people to recognize the freedom of others—had been influential for me. So had its form, a series of letters, addressed in Schiller's case to a Danish prince, in which he hoped to bring together the "power of abstraction" and the "power of the imagination" in an "equal tension." As someone who toggles back and forth between writing critical essays and fiction, this in-between space has always been generative for me. Schiller's self-description also struck a chord: "I hover, like a kind of hybrid, between concept and contemplation, between law and feeling. […] It is this that gave me […] a somewhat awkward appearance both in the field of speculation and in that of poetry."[1] His in-between-ness as a thinker and a writer gave me confidence in my own "awkward appearance," or at least enough to begin.

Another model was Marcuse's *Essay on Liberation,* published in 1969, his attempt to think through the turning point of the late sixties when the "new sensibility" emerged, combining a great

---

1 Friedrich Schiller, *On the Aesthetic Education of Man,* trans. Reginald Snell (Kettering: Angelico Press, 2014), 5.

refusal of the existing system of values with a willingness to struggle for new ways and forms of life. It gave me the freedom to write this love letter to our own moment, and to undertake to understand by way of autonomy the forms, feelings and solidarities that have emerged in the last decade or so that seemed impossible in the three decades before. Still another example I followed was the revolutionary communiqués of the Zapatistas, written from deep within the autonomous imaginary.

And, like a sign, as I was finishing the first draft of this book in August of 2019, a new letter arrived from the Lacondon Jungle, addressed, as the Zapatistas' letters always are, to anyone open to receiving it. It contained the startling pronouncement that the revolutionaries had expanded their autonomous regions in Chiapas from five original Centres of Autonomous Resistance and Rebellion to twelve. Despite ongoing counterinsurgency campaigns, both military and social, by the Mexican government, and the launch of several neoliberal megaprojects in the region — the "Maya" train, the Trans-Isthmus Corridor and the Project Sembrando Vida — the Zapatistas had nevertheless managed to self-organize over five hundred thousand people in the remote mountains of Chiapas, with their own system of education, health, justice, government, and security, all rooted in radically democratic processes.

This communiqué marked a significant development in Zapatista history — perhaps the most significant since the formation of the first Caracoles in 2003. And as letters (especially Zapatista communiqués) do, it clarified our moment. It spoke of being under siege, and in the same breath of having broken the siege: "We defeated the government's siege of our communities — it did not work and it will never work. [...] [W]e understood that the walls that are built and the sieges laid only bring death."[2] A January communiqué from Zapatista women to women in struggle around the world, had described the situation even more baldly: "Capitalism is coming for us, for eve-

---

2 "Communique from the EZLN's CCRI-CG: And We Broke the Siege," *Radio Zapatista*, August 17, 2019, https://radiozapatista.org/?p=32087&lang=en.

rything, and at any price. This assault is now possible because those in power feel that many people support them and will applaud them no matter what barbarities they carry out."[3]

The point of the August 2019 letter was not only to share the news that in the face of this siege (a version of which we too are under), the Zapatistas had grown in size and strength, but also to invite us to break the siege on the radical imagination and to grow our autonomies within the context of an international network of rebellion and resistance. "This Network," it stated, "should be based on the independence and autonomy of those who constitute it, explicitly renouncing all attempts at hegemony or homogeny, where mutual aid is unconditional and all share in each other's good and bad experiences, all the while working to circulate all the histories of the struggles that take place below and to the left."[4]

That invitation was accompanied by another to "those who have dedicated their life and their livelihood to art, science, and critical thought" to join in festivals, encounters, fiestas, exchanges, and "seedbeds."[5] Such encounters have always been central to the Zapatistas' work of radical imagining, but the letter announced new plans to host encounters between the families of the "murdered, disappeared, and imprisoned" and the organizations, groups, and collectives dedicated to assisting them; between Zapatista women and women in struggle around the world; and between *otroas,* the Zapatista word for LGBTQ+ people, to share and organize around their experiences.[6] Reading this call, I wondered, what if we were actually to try to form the international autonomous network the Zapatistas are calling for, and which they continually seek to activate across the

---

[3] "Letter from the Zapatista Women to Women in Struggle Around the World," *Enlace Zapatista,* February 13, 2019, https://enlacezapatista.ezln.org.mx/2019/02/13/letter-from-the-zapatista-women-to-women-in-struggle-around-the-world/.

[4] "Communique from the EZLN's CCRI-CG."

[5] Ibid.

[6] Ibid.

spheres of politics, art, science and critical thought?[7] What if we were to become more imaginative, not less, in response to the global turn toward heteronomy? What if, as Staughton Lynd once said, the Zapatistas have been where we are going?[8]

But it doesn't have to happen that way — there are any number of roads we can take, and of course I know we aren't entirely free to choose which road and when. I know that we are *barely* free; dialectics are helpful for reminding us of that. But what a dialectician might call "voluntarism," I would call *libido formandi*, after Castoriadis, the desire for creation, which accompanies *vis formandi*, the power *of* creation. This must exist, for without it we would be frozen in place — or ground to dust.

Autonomy is a political project that understands history and society as continually creative formations *in each and every moment*, hence its capacity to augment our ability to struggle. Insofar as it connects the contents of the individual psyche to the social imaginary, it's the only political project to which art is central and the only political project that is central to art. As the Black radical tradition has shown us, the politics of art's autonomy go beyond liberal democratic activism on behalf of freedom of speech or Marxist monitoring of the machinery of capital. They call existing institutions into question, including the institution of art, *and* create or help to create new modes of instituting. For the autonomy project is not just about challenging the status quo, as Castoriadis reminds us, "it is also, in light of this interrogation, to make, to do and to institute."[9]

---

[7] Art, culture and education also play a central role in the Rojavan autonomy project. See Dilar Dirik, "Stateless Citizenship: 'Radical Democracy as Consciousness-raising' in the Rojava Revolution," *Identities* 29, no. 1 (2022): 27–44.

[8] Staughton Lynd and Andrej Grubačić, *Wobblies and Zapatistas: Conversations on Anarchism, Marxism and Radical History* (Oakland: PM Press, 2008), 50.

[9] Cornelius Castoriadis, "Power, Politics, Autonomy," in *Philosophy, Politics, Autonomy: Essays in Political Philosophy*, ed. David Ames Curtis (Oxford: Oxford University Press, 1991), 164.

Nine months on, as I finish another draft, it feels as if a new world has been born — not a world where everything is different, but a world where people are once more willing to struggle to make everything different. Autonomy is all around us again: in the worldwide Black Lives Matter protests in response to George Floyd's murder, which have a one-time-too-many-times feel to them, a refusal of all that is; in the renewed effort to confront America's foundational myth of white supremacy and every structure it inhabits; in the mutual aid practices springing up to meet the challenge of COVID-19 and police crackdowns against protesters (including the declaration of autonomous zones in Seattle (CHAP) and Philadelphia (Camp Maroon); in the skepticism towards the corporate "solidarity" statements spilling out all over; in the feeling that the meaning of everything has shifted.

When activity like this takes place on a grand scale, it ushers in what Castoriadis calls an "instituting socio-historical moment," which is to say, "the bringing about of a history in which society not only knows itself, but makes itself."[10] Is this where we find ourselves today? Certainly we're experiencing solidarity as a creative force. And who knows what part the coronavirus lockdown played in all of this? When everyday life under capitalism "closed down," did it make another way of living seem possible? Other lives have value? Did losing our ability to see and touch friends and loved ones make us value — and want to fight for — those ties above all else? Did the callous endangerment of the lives of nurses, delivery drivers and supermarket employees make capitalism's war on workers more legible? Did the closing of schools make the needs of children and parents, especially primary caregivers, more visible? Did the shuttering of workplaces cause a rethinking of what work is — and what it should be?

As I write this in May of 2020, it is safer to join a protest (with a mask) than to return to "normal" (shopping, dining, drinking without one). As with all autonomous movements, this one

---

10 Ibid.

has the potential to transform the whole of society. Certainly, a backlash is already forming (it was always already there), but as monuments to white supremacy fall all over the world, alongside laws upholding police brutality and budgets enabling police militarization, each new day brings some jaw-dropping translation of the potential into the actual.

What will art institutions become if and when they reopen? Will the politics of art's autonomy rise to the occasion? Yale Union's recent transfer of ownership of its land and historic building to the Native Arts and Cultures Foundation in Portland suggests that art spaces may be ready — or should be ready — to take on new meanings. If "the spotless gallery wall [...] is in the image of the society that supports it," then what would different spaces occupied by different bodies in a different society look like?[11] How will artists further autonomize the institution of art through their formal, social, and political practices? What part will they play in this other re-opening, which right now outstrips that of the economy — the reopening of the radical social imaginary? All these questions remain to be answered, dear A — dear Artist, dear Activist, dear Academic, dear Autonomist — and more will follow. Autonomy is never an end, but always a beginning.

---

11 Brian O'Dougherty, *Inside the White Cube: The Ideology of the Gallery Space* (Santa Monica: Lapis Press, 1976), 79.

Bibliography

"A Conversation with Theodor W. Adorno (*Spiegel,* 1969)." *Communists in Situ,* September 1, 2015. https://cominsitu.wordpress.com/2015/09/01/a-conversation-with-theodor-w-adorno-spiegel-1969/.

Adler, Judith. *Artists in Offices: An Ethnography of an Academic Art Scene.* New York: Routledge, 2017.

Adorno, Theodor. *Aesthetic Theory.* Translated by Robert Hullot-Kentor. Minneapolis: University of Minnesota Press, 1996.

———. *Negative Dialectics.* London: Taylor and Francis e-Library, 2004.

Adorno, Theodor, and Herbert Marcuse. "Correspondence on the German Student Movement." Translated by Esther Leslie. *New Left Review* I/233 (January-February 1999): 123–36.

"An Interview with Fred Moten, Pt. II." *Literary Hub,* August 6, 2015. https://lithub.com/an-interview-with-fred-moten-pt-ii/.

Atlas, Caron. "Radical Imagination." In *Beyond Zuccotti Park: Freedom of Assembly and the Occupation of Public Space,* edited by Ron Shiffman, 146–55. Oakland: New Village Press, 2012.

Baldessari, John. "Reflections." In *Jack Goldstein and the CalArts Mafia,* edited by Richard Herz, 59–68. Ojai: Minneola Press, 2003.

Bambara, Toni Cade. "On the Issue of Roles." In *The Black Woman: An Anthology,* edited by Toni Cade Bambara, 101–10. Ann Arbor: University of Michigan Press, 1970.

———, ed. *The Black Woman: An Anthology.* Ann Arbor: University of Michigan Press, 1970.

Baraka, Amiri. *Black Magic: Sabotage, Target Study, Black Art: Collected Poetry 1961–1967.* Indianapolis: Bobbs-Merrill, 1969.

Beck, Julian. *The Life of the Theatre.* Ann Arbor: University of Michigan Press, 2008.

Becker, Howard. *Art Worlds.* Berkeley: University of California Press, 1982.

Beech, Dave. *Art and Value: Art's Economic Exceptionalism in Classical, Neoclassical and Marxist Economics.* Chicago: Haymarket, 2015.

Berlant, Lauren. "Cruel Optimism." In *The Affect Theory Reader,* edited by Melissa Gregg and Gregory J. Seigworth, 93–117. Durham: Duke University Press, 2010.

Bishop, Claire. *Artificial Hells: Participatory Art and the Politics of Spectatorship.* London: Verso, 2011.

———. "Participation as Spectacle: Where Are We Now?" In *Living as Form: Socially Engaged Art From 1991–2011,* edited by Nato Thompson, 34–45. New York: Creative Time, 2012.

Blau, Herbert. "Disney's Dough Takes Flight." March 7, 1970. Berkeley, CA. KPFA radio broadcast.

Bracey, John H. "The Questions We Should Be Asking: Introduction to the 2006 Edition." In C.L.R. James and Grace C. Lee, with the collaboration of Cornelius Castoriadis, *Facing Reality: The New Society: Where to Look for It and How to Bring It Closer,* 1–8. Chicago: Charles H. Kerr, 2006.

Bracey, John H., Jr., Sonia Sanchez, and James Smethurst. "Editors' Introduction." In *SOS–Calling All Black People:*

A Black Arts Movement Reader, edited by John H. Bracey Jr., Sonia Sanchez, and James Smethurst, 1–10. Amherst: University of Massachusetts Press, 2014.

Brawer, Wendy E., and Brennan S. Cavanaugh. "Being There." In *Beyond Zuccotti Park: Freedom of Assembly and the Occupation of Public Space, edited by Ron Shiffman*, 49–60. Oakland: New Village Press, 2012.

Bretteville, Sheila de, Barry Hyams, and Marianne Partridge, eds. *Arts in Society* 7, no. 3, Special Issue: "California Institute of the Arts: Prologue to a Community" (Fall–Winter 1970). https://digicoll.library.wisc.edu/cgi-bin/Arts/Arts-idx?id=Arts.ArtsSocv07i3

Brown, Nicholas. *Autonomy: The Social Ontology of Art under Capitalism*. Durham: Duke University Press, 2019.

Brown, Scot. "The US Organization, Black Power Vanguard Politics, and the United Front Ideal: Los Angeles and Beyond." *Black Scholar* 31, no. 3/4 (Fall/Winter 2001): 21–30.

———. "The US Organization, Maulana Karenga, and Conflict with the Black Panther Party: A Critique of Sectarian Influences on Historical Discourse." *Journal of Black Studies* 28, no. 2 (November 1997): 157–70.

Burger, Peter. *Theory of the Avant-Garde*. Minneapolis: University of Minnesota Press, 1984.

CalArts Admissions Bulletin 1969–1970, Series 12.1, CalArts Publications 1963–87, CalArts Archive, California Institute of the Arts, Valencia, California.

Carmichael, Stokely. "Black Power (1960)." *Black Past*, July 13, 2010. https://www.blackpast.org/african-american-history/1966-stokely-carmichael-black-power/.

Carroll, Nicole. "Tarana Burke on the Power of Empathy: The Building Block of the Me Too Movement." *USA Today*, August 19, 2020. https://www.usatoday.com/in-depth/life/women-of-the-century/2020/08/19/tarana-burke-me-too-movement-19th-amendment-women-of-century/5535976002/.

Castoriadis, Cornelius. "An Interview." *Radical Philosophy* 56 (Autumn 1990): 35–43.

———. "Culture in a Democratic Society." In *The Castoriadis Reader*, edited and translated by David Ames Curtis, 338–48. Oxford: Blackwell, 1997.

———. "Democracy as Procedure, Democracy as Regime." In *The Rising Tide of Insignificancy (The Big Sleep)*, translated and edited anonymously as a public service, 329–62. N.p.: Not Bored [2003]. http://www.notbored.org/RTI.pdf.

———. "From Ecology to Autonomy." In *The Castoriadis Reader*, edited and translated by David Ames Curtis, 236–52. Oxford: Blackwell, 1997.

———. "Marxism and Revolutionary Theory: Excerpts." In *The Castoriadis Reader*, edited and translated by David Ames Curtis, 139–95. Oxford: Blackwell, 1997.

———. *Philosophy, Politics, Autonomy: Essays in Political Philosophy*. Edited by David Ames Curtis. Oxford: Oxford University Press, 1991.

———. "Physis and Autonomy." In *World in Fragments: Writings on Politics, Society, Psychoanalysis, and the Imagination*, edited and translated by David Ames Curtis, 331–41. Stanford: Stanford University Press, 1997.

———. *Political and Social Writings*, Vol. 1: *1946–1955: From the Critique of Bureaucracy to the Positive Content of Socialism*. Translated and edited by David Ames Curtis. Minneapolis: University of Minnesota Press, 1988.

———. "Power, Politics, Autonomy." In *Philosophy, Politics, Autonomy: Essays in Political Philosophy*, edited by David Ames Curtis, 143–74. Oxford: Oxford University Press, 1991.

———. "Primal Institution of Society and Second-Order Institutions." In *Figures of the Thinkable*, translated by Helen Arnold, 91–104. Stanford: Stanford University Press, 2007.

———. "Psychoanalysis and Politics." In *World in Fragments: Writings on Politics, Society, Psychoanalysis, and the Imagination*, edited and translated by David Ames Curtis, 125–36. Stanford: Stanford University Press, 1997.

———. "Radical Imagination and the Social Instituting Imaginary." In *The Castoriadis Reader*, edited and translated by David Ames Curtis, 319–37. Oxford: Blackwell, 1997.

———. "Recommencing the Revolution." In *The Castoriadis Reader*, edited and translated by David Ames Curtis, 106–38. Oxford: Blackwell, 1997.

———. "The Dilapidation of the West." In *The Rising Tide of Insignificancy (The Big Sleep)*, translated and edited anonymously as a public service, 73–108. N.p.: Not Bored [2003]. http://www.notbored.org/RTI.pdf.

———. "The Greek and the Modern Political Imaginary." In *World in Fragments: Writings on Politics, Society, Psychoanalysis, and the Imagination*, edited and translated by David Ames Curtis, 84–107. Stanford: Stanford University Press, 1997.

———. "The Idea of Revolution (1989)." In *The Rising Tide of Insignificancy (The Big Sleep)*, translated and edited anonymously as a public service, 288–310. N.p.: Not Bored [2003]. http://www.notbored.org/RTI.pdf.

———. "The Imaginary: Creation in the Socio-Historical Domain." In *World in Fragments: Writings on Politics, Society, Psychoanalysis, and the Imagination*, edited and translated by David Ames Curtis, 3–18. Stanford: Stanford University Press, 1997.

———. *The Imaginary Institution of Society*. Cambridge: MIT Press, 1998.

———. "The Movements of the Sixties." In *World in Fragments: Writings on Politics, Society, Psychoanalysis, and the Imagination*, edited and translated by David Ames Curtis, 47–57. Stanford: Stanford University Press, 1997.

———. "The Only Way to Find Out If You Can Swim Is to Get into the Water: An Introductory Interview." In *The Castoriadis Reader*, edited and translated by David Ames Curtis, 1–34. Oxford: Blackwell, 1997.

———. "The Pulverization of Marxism-Leninism." In *World in Fragments: Writings on Politics, Society, Psychoanalysis, and the Imagination,* edited and translated by David Ames Curtis, 58–69. Stanford: Stanford University Press, 1997.

———. "The Revolutionary Force of Ecology." In *The Rising Tide of Insignificancy (The Big Sleep),* translated and edited anonymously as a public service, 109–23. N.p.: Not Bored [2003]. http://www.notbored.org/RTI.pdf.

Ciccariello-Maher, George. *Decolonizing Dialectics.* Durham: Duke University Press, 2017.

Clover, Joshua. *Riot. Strike. Riot: The New Era of Uprisings.* London: Verso, 2016.

Cohn-Bendit, Daniel, and Gabriel Cohn-Bendit. *Obsolete Communism: The Left-Wing Alternative.* Translated by Arnold Pomerans. London: André Deutsch, 1968.

"Communique from the EZLN's CCRI-CG: And We Broke the Siege." *Radio Zapatista,* August 17, 2019. https://radiozapatista.org/?p=32087&lang=en.

Cruse, Harold. "The Harlem Black Arts Theater–New Dialogue with the Lost Black Generation." In *SOS–Calling All Black People: A Black Arts Movement Reader,* edited by John H. Bracey Jr., Sonia Sanchez, and James Smethurst, 39–45. Amherst: University of Massachusetts Press, 2014.

Curtis, David Ames. "Cornelius Castoriadis: An Obituary." *Salmagundi* 118/119 (Spring–Summer 1998): 56.

Dean, Jodi. "Occupation as Political Form." *Occupy Everything,* April 12, 2012. http://occupyeverything.org/2012/occupation-as-political-form/.

Diehl, Travis. "Op-ed: An Ultra-red Line." *X-tra Online,* October 12, 2017. https://www.x-traonline.org/online/travis-diehl-op-ed-an-ultra-red-line/.

———. "White-Wall White." *East of Borneo,* October 12, 2017. https://eastofborneo.org/articles/white-wall-white/.

Dirik, Dilar. "Stateless Citizenship: 'Radical Democracy as Consciousness-raising' in the Rojava Revolution." *Identities* 29, no. 1 (2022): 27–44. DOI: 10.1080/1070289X.2021.1970978.

Duggan, Lisa. "The Full Catastrophe." *Bully Bloggers,* August 18, 2018. https://bullybloggers.wordpress.com/2018/08/18/the-full-catastrophe/.

———. "Optimistic Cruelty." *Social Text,* January 15, 2013. http://socialtextjournal.org/periscope_article/optimistic-cruelty/.

Endnotes. "A History of Separation: The Defeat of the Workers Movement." *Endnotes* 4: "Unity and Separation" (2015). https://endnotes.org.uk/issues/4/en/endnotes-the-defeat-of-the-workers-movement.

———."Brown v. Ferguson." *Endnotes* 4: "Unity and Separation" (2015). https://endnotes.org.uk/issues/4/en/endnotes-brown-v-ferguson.

———. "Communisation and Value Form Theory: Introduction." *Endnotes* 2: "Misery and the Value Form" (2010). https://endnotes.org.uk/issues/2/en/endnotes-communisation-and-value-form-theory.

———. "What Are We to Do?" In *Communization and Its Discontents: Contestation, Critique and Contemporary Struggles,* edited by Benjamin Noys, 23–40. New York: Minor Compositions, 2012.

Estes, Nick. *Our History Is the Future: Standing Rock versus the Dakota Access Pipeline, and the Long Tradition of Indigenous Resistance.* London: Verso, 2019.

Federal Bureau of Investigation, United States Department of Justice. *US* (April 1968). https://www.governmentattic.org/docs/FBI_Monograph_US_April-1968.pdf.

Federici, Sylvia, and Arlen Austin, eds. *Wages for Housework: The New York Wages for Housework Committee 1972–1973: History, Theory and Documents.* Brooklyn: Autonomedia, 2017.

Fotopoulos, Takis. "From (Mis)education to Paideia." *International Journal of Inclusive Democracy* 2, no. 1 (September 2005). https://www.inclusivedemocracy.org/journal/vol2/vol2_no1_miseducation_paideia_takis.htm.

Fragoza, Caribbean. "Art and Complicity: How the Fight against Gentrification in Boyle Heights Questions the Role of Artists." *KCET,* July 20, 2016. https://www.kcet.org/shows/artbound/boyle-heights-gentrification-art-galleries-pssst.

Freire, Paolo. *Pedagogy of the Oppressed*. Translated by Myra Bergman Ramos. London: Bloomsbury Academic, 2000.

Fukuyama, Francis. *The End of History and the Last Man*. New York: Free Press, 1992.

Garza, Alicia, and Patrisse Cullors-Brignac. "Celebrating MLK Day: Reclaiming Our Movement Legacy." *Huffington Post*, March 20, 2015. https://www.huffpost.com/entry/reclaiming-our-movement-l_b_6498400.

Gavroche, Julius. "Jacques Rancière: The Anarchy of Democracy." *Autonomies*, May 10, 2017. https://autonomies.org/2017/05/jacques-ranciere-the-anarchy-of-democracy/.

Gerald, Carolyn. "Symposium: The Measure and the Meaning of the Sixties." In *SOS–Calling All Black People: A Black Arts Movement Reader*, edited by John H. Bracey Jr., Sonia Sanchez, and James Smethurst, 46–50. Amherst: University of Massachusetts Press, 2014.

Gleeson, Jules Joanne, and Elle O'Rourke. "Introduction." In *Transgender Marxism*, edited by Jules Joanne Gleeson and Elle O'Rourke, 1–32. London: Pluto, 2021.

Golan, Gan. "The Office of the People." In *Beyond Zuccotti Park: Freedom of Assembly and the Occupation of Public Space*, edited by Ron Shiffman, 70–73. Oakland: New Village Press, 2012.

Graeber, David. "Occupy Wall Street's Anarchist Roots." *Al Jazeera*, November 30, 2011. https://www.aljazeera.com/opinions/2011/11/30/occupy-wall-streets-anarchist-roots.

Haiman, Franklyn S. "The Rhetoric of the Streets: Some Legal and Ethical Considerations." *Quarterly Journal of Speech* 53, no. 2 (1967): 99–114. DOI: 10.1080/00335636709382822.

Halperin, Julia. "The Four Glass Ceilings: How Women Artists Get Stiffed at Every Stage of Their Careers." *Artnet*, December 15, 2017. https://news.artnet.com/market/art-market-study-1179317.

Harcourt, Bernard E. "Political Disobedience." In W.J.T. Mitchell, Bernard E. Harcourt, and Michael Taussig, *Occupy: Three Inquiries in Disobedience*, 3–44. Chicago: University of Chicago Press, 2013.

Harney, Stefano, and Fred Moten. *The Undercommons: Fugitive Planning and Black Study.* New York: Minor Compositions 2013.

Harrington, Michael. "Marxism and Democracy." *Praxis International* 1, no. 1 (April 1981). Available at *Palinurus: Engaging Political Philosophy,* https://anselmocarranco.tripod.com/id25.html.

Hastings-King, Stephen. "L'Internationale Situationniste, Socialisme ou Barbarie, and the Crisis of the Marxist Imaginary." *SubStance* 28, no. 3, Special Issue: "Guy Debord," edited by Pierpaolo Antonello and Olga Vasile (1999): 26–54. DOI: 10.1353/sub.2006.0007.

Herz, Richard, ed. *Jack Goldstein and the CalArts Mafia.* Ojai: Minneola Press, 2003.

Higgins, Hannah. *Fluxus Experience.* Berkeley: University of California Press, 2002.

Hilliard, David, and Donald Weise, eds. *The Huey P. Newton Reader.* New York: Seven Stories, 2002.

Illich, Ivan. *Deschooling Society.* London: Marion Boyars, 1971.

James, C.L.R., and Grace C. Lee, with the collaboration of Cornelius Castoriadis. *Facing Reality: The New Society: Where to Look for It and How to Bring It Closer.* Chicago: Charles H. Kerr, 2006.

James, Selma. *Sex, Race and Class, The Perspective of Winning: A Selection of Writings 1952–2011.* Oakland: PM Press, 2012.

Jameson, Fredric. *Archaeologies of the Future: The Desire Called Utopia and Other Science Fictions.* London: Verso, 2005.

Jones, Meta DuEwa. "Politics, Process and (Jazz) Performance: Amiri Baraka's 'It's Nation Time.'" *African American Review* 37, no. 2/3 (Summer–Autumn, 2003): 245–52. DOI: 10.1632/S0030812921000195.

Karenga, Ron. "Black Cultural Nationalism." In *SOS-Calling All Black People: A Black Arts Movement Reader,* edited by John H. Bracey Jr., Sonia Sanchez, and James Smethurst, 51–54. Amherst: University of Massachusetts Press, 2014.

Katsiaficas, Georgy. *The Subversion of Politics: European Autonomous Movements and the Decolonization of Everyday Life*. Oakland: AK Press, 2006.

Kester, Grant. *Conversation Pieces: Community and Communication in Modern Art*. Berkeley: University of California Press, 2004.

———. "On the Relationship between Theory and Practice in Socially Engaged Art." *A Blade of Grass*, July 29, 2015. https://abladeofgrass.org/fertile-ground/on-the-relationship-between-theory-and-practice-in-socially-engaged-art/.

———. *The One and the Many: Contemporary Collaborative Art in a Global Setting*. Durham: Duke University Press, 2011.

———. "The Sound of Breaking Glass, Part II: Agonism and the Taming of Dissent." *e-flux* 31 (January 2012). http://www.e-flux.com/journal/the-sound-of-breaking-glass-part-ii-agonism-and-the-taming-of-dissent/.

Klein, Naomi. "Occupy Wall Street: The Most Important Thing in the World Now." *The Nation*, October 6, 2011. http://www.thenation.com/article/163844/occupy-wall-street-most-important-thing-world-now.

Kliman, Andrew. "The Make-Believe World of David Graeber." *Marxist Humanities Initiative,* April 13, 2012. http://www.marxisthumanistinitiative.org/alternatives-to-capital/the-make-believe-world-of-david-graeber.html.

Knight, Christopher. "A Situation Where Art Might Happen: John Baldesarri on CalArts." *East of Borneo*, November 19, 2011. https://eastofborneo.org/articles/a-situation-where-art-might-happen-john-baldessari-on-calarts/.

Kroll, Andy. "How Occupy Wall Street Really Got Started." *Mother Jones*, October 17, 2017. http://www.motherjones.com/politics/2011/10/occupy-wall-street-international-origins.

"Laura Owens Responds to Protests of 356 S. Mission Rd." *Artforum International*, November 14, 2017. https://www.

artforum.com/news/laura-owens-responds-to-protests-of-356-s-mission-rd-72259.

"Letter from the Zapatista Women to Women in Struggle Around the World." *Enlace Zapatista,* February 13, 2019. https://enlacezapatista.ezln.org.mx/2019/02/13/letter-from-the-zapatista-women-to-women-in-struggle-around-the-world/.

Lonzi, Carla. "Let's Spit on Hegel." In *Italian Feminist Thought: A Reader,* edited by Paola Bono and Sandra Kemp, 40–58. London: Basil Blackwell, 1991.

Lotringer, Sylvère, and Christian Marazzi. "The Return of Politics." In *Autonomia: Post-Political Politics,* edited by Sylvère Lotringer and Christian Marazzi, 8–23. Los Angeles: Semiotext(e), 2007.

Lynd, Staughton, and Andrej Grubačić. *Wobblies and Zapatistas: Conversations on Anarchism, Marxism and Radical History.* Oakland: PM Press, 2008.

MacKenzie, Catriona, and Natalie Stoljar, eds. *Relational Autonomy: Feminist Perspectives on Autonomy, Agency and the Social Self.* Oxford: Oxford University Press, 2000.

MacPherson, C.B. *The Political Theory of Possessive Individualism: Hobbes to Locke.* Oxford: Oxford University Press, 2011.

Made in China Journal. "Stefano Harney, Fred Moten, and Michael Sawyer: 'On Fugitive Aesthetics.'" *Youtube,* March 15, 2021. https://youtu.be/iBJh-9caNf4.

Malcolm X. "Message to the Grassroots (1963)." *Black Past,* August 16, 2010. https://www.blackpast.org/african-american-history/speeches-african-american-history/1963-malcolm-x-message-grassroots/.

Marcuse, Herbert. "Art as Form of Reality." In *Art and Liberation,* 140–48. Collected Papers of Marcuse 4. London: Routledge, 2006.

———. *Essay on Liberation.* Boston: Beacon, 1969.

———. "Herbert Marcuse and the Student Revolts of 1968: An Unpublished Lecture." *Jacobin,* March 2021. https://

jacobinmag.com/2021/03/herbert-marcuse-student-revolts-of-1968-ucsd-lecture.

———. *One-Dimensional Man: Studies in the Ideology of Advanced Industrial Society.* 1964; repr. Boston: Beacon, 2012

———. *The Aesthetic Dimension: Toward a Critique of Marxist Aesthetics.* Boston: Beacon, 1977.

Martin, Bradford. "Politics as Art, Art as Politics: The Freedom Singers, the Living Theatre and Public Performance." In *Long Time Gone: Sixties America Then and Now,* edited by Alexander Bloom, 159-88. Oxford: Oxford University Press, 2001.

———. *The Theater Is in the Street: Politics and Public Performance in 1960s America.* Amherst: University of Massachusetts Press, 2004.

McAndrew, Claire. "Why the 'Superstar Economics' of the Art Market Is Its Biggest Threat." *Artsy,* November 27, 2017. https://www.artsy.net/article/artsy-editorial-superstar-economics-art-market-threat.

McKee, Yates. *Strike Art: Contemporary Art and the Post-Occupy Condition.* London: Verso, 2016.

Milan Women's Bookshop Collective. *Sexual Difference: A Theory of Social-Symbolic Practice.* Translated by Patrizia Cicogna and Teresa de Lauretis. Bloomington: Indiana University Press, 1990.

Miranda, Carolina A. "'Out!' Boyle Heights Activists Say White Art Elites Are Ruining the Neighborhood … But It's Complicated." *Los Angeles Times,* October 14, 2016. https://www.latimes.com/entertainment/arts/miranda/la-et-cam-art-gentrification-boyle-heights-20161014-snap-story.html.

Miranda, Magally, and Kyle Lane-McKinley. "Artwashing, or, Between Social Practice and Social Reproduction." *A Blade of Grass,* February 1, 2017. http://www.abladeofgrass.org/fertile-ground/artwashing-social-practice-social-reproduction/.

Mitchell, William. "Image, Space, Revolution: The Arts of Occupation." In W.J.T. Mitchell, Bernard E. Harcourt, and Michael Taussig, *Occupy: Three Inquiries in Disobedience*, 93–129. Chicago: University of Chicago Press, 2013.

MSNBC. "Queerness on the Front Lines of #BlackLivesMatter | Original | msnbc." *YouTube*, February 20, 2015. https://www.youtube.com/watch?v=0YHs9jIH-00.

Neal, Larry. "The Black Arts Movement." In *SOS–Calling All Black People: A Black Arts Movement Reader*, edited by John H. Bracey Jr., Sonia Sanchez, and James Smethurst, 55–66. Amherst: University of Massachusetts Press, 2014.

Negri, Toni. "Domination and Sabotage." In *Autonomia: Post-Political Politics*, edited by Sylvère Lotringer and Christian Marazzi, 62–71. Los Angeles: Semiotext(e), 2007.

Newton, Huey P. "Intercommunalism (1974)." *Viewpoint Magazine*, June 11, 2018. https://www.viewpointmag.com/2018/06/11/intercommunalism-1974/.

———. "The Women's Liberation and Gay Liberation Movements (1970)." *Black Past*, April 17, 2018. https://www.blackpast.org/african-american-history/speeches-african-american-history/huey-p-newton-women-s-liberation-and-gay-liberation-movements/.

———. "Uniting Against a Common Enemy: October 13, 1971." In *The Huey P. Newton Reader*, edited by David Hilliard and Donald Weise, 234–40. New York: Seven Stories, 2002.

Noys, Benjamin, ed. *Malign Velocities.* Winchester: Zero Books, 2014.

O'Dougherty, Brian. *Inside the White Cube: The Ideology of the Gallery Space.* Santa Monica: Lapis Press, 1976.

Petsche, Jackson. "The Importance of Being Autonomous: Toward a Marxist Defense of Art for Art's Sake." *Mediations: Journal of the Marxist Literary Group* 26, nos. 1–2 (Fall–Spring 2013): 143–58. https://www.mediationsjournal.org/articles/the-importance-of-being-autonomous.

Pogrebin, Robin, and Elizabeth A. Harris. "Warren Kanders Quits Whitney Board after Tear Gas Protests." *The New York*

Times, July 25, 2019. https://www.nytimes.com/2019/07/25/arts/whitney-warren-kanders-resigns.html.

Raha, Nat. "The Limits of Trans Liberalism." *Verso Books* (blog), September 21, 2015. https://www.versobooks.com/blogs/2245-the-limits-of-trans-liberalism-by-nat-raha.

Rancière, Jacques. *Aesthetics and Its Discontents.* Translated by Steven Corcoran. Cambridge: Polity, 2009.

———. *Dissensus: On Politics and Aesthetics.* Edited and translated Steven Corcoran. London: Bloomsbury 2010

———. "The Distribution of the Sensible: Politics and Aesthetics." In *The Politics of Aesthetics: The Distribution of the Sensible,* edited by Gabriel Rockhill, 12–19. London: Continuum, 2004.

———. *The Emancipated Spectator.* Translated by Gregory Elliot. London: Verso, 2011.

———. "The Paradoxes of Political Art." In *Dissensus: On Politics and Aesthetics,* edited and translated Steven Corcoran, 134–51. London: Bloomsbury 2010.

———. *The Politics of Aesthetics: The Distribution of the Sensible.* Edited by Gabriel Rockhill. London: Continuum, 2004

Raven, Arlene. "Womanhouse." In *The Power of Feminist Art,* edited by Judith Brodsky, Norma Broude, and Mary Garraude, 48–65. New York: Harry Abrams, 1994.

"Reagan Interview in Sacramento, Part II." *KQED News,* January 16, 1969. San Francisco State University, Academic Technology Archives, Diva. 17:45. https://diva.sfsu.edu/collections/sfbatv/bundles/187218.

Rios, Michael. "Emplacing Democratic Design." In *Beyond Zuccotti Park: Freedom of Assembly and the Occupation of Public Space,* edited by Ron Shiffman, 133–42. Oakland: New Village Press, 2012.

Rockhill, Gabriel. *Radical History and the Politics of Art.* New York: Columbia University Press, 2014.

———. "Rancière's Productive Contradictions: From the Politics of Aesthetics to the Social Politicity of Artistic Practice." *Symposium* 15, no. 2 (Fall 2011): 28–56.

Rosenthal, Tracy Jeanne. "Contributor Tracy Jeanne Rosenthal Responds to Laura Owens." *Daily Gentrifier,* November 27, 2017. https://thedailygentrifier.com/news/2017/11/27/tracy-rosenthal-responds-to-laura-owens-la-artwashing (site discontinued).

Rosler, Martha. "Culture Class: Art, Creativity, Urbanism, Part II." *e-flux* 23 (March, 2011). https://www.e-flux.com/journal/23/67813/culture-class-art-creativity-urbanism-part-ii/.

Roth, Moira. "Suzanne Lacy on the Feminist Art Program at Fresno and Calarts." *East of Borneo,* December 15, 2011. https://eastofborneo.org/articles/suzanne-lacy-on-the-feminist-program-at-fresno-state-and-calarts.

Sanchez, Sonia. *We a BaddDDD People.* Detroit: Broadside Press, 1973.

Sarbanes, Janet. "A School Based on What Artists Wanted to Do: Alison Knowles on CalArts." *East of Borneo,* August 7, 2012. https://eastofborneo.org/articles/a-school-based-on-what-artists-wanted-to-do-alison-knowles-on-calarts/.

———. "Teaching (Which Is Not Teaching) Art (Which Is Not Art)." In *Where Art Might Happen: The Early Years of Calarts,* edited by Philipp Kaiser and Christina Vegh, 155–68. Munich: Prestel Publishing, 2021.

Sayej, Nadja. "Alyssa Milano on the #MeToo Movement: 'We're Not Going to Stand for It Any More.'" *The Guardian,* December 1, 2017. https://www.theguardian.com/culture/2017/dec/01/alyssa-milano-mee-too-sexual-harassment-abuse.

Schiller, Friedrich. *On the Aesthetic Education of Man.* Translated by Reginald Snell. Kettering: Angelico Press, 2014.

Schmidt, Samantha. "Fireworks Tragedy: The 'Magical' Mexican Town Where Pyrotechnics Are Life—and Too Often Death." *Houston Chronicle,* December 21, 2016. http://www.chron.com/news/nation-world/world/article/Fireworks-tragedy-The-magical-Mexican-town-10811226.php.

Shaked, Nizan. "How to Draw a (Picket) Line: Activists Protest Event at Boyle Heights Gallery." *Hyperallergic,* February 14, 2017. https://hyperallergic.com/358652/how-to-draw-a-picket-line-activists-protest-event-at-boyle-heights-gallery/.

———. "Why I Am Resigning from X-TRA Contemporary Art Quarterly and the Problem with 356 Mission's Politics." *Hyperallergic,* April 27, 2018. https://hyperallergic.com/440234/x-tra-contemporary-art-quarterly-356-mission-boyle-heights/.

Shahvisi, Arianne. "Beyond Orientalism: Exploring the Distinctive Feminism of Democratic Confederalism in Rojava." *Sussex Research Online.* http://sro.sussex.ac.uk/id/eprint/80502/.

Sholette, Gregory. "Some Call It Art: From Imaginary Autonomy to Autonomous Collectivity." *Subsol.* http://subsol.c3.hu/subsol_2/contributors3/sholettetext.html.

Simmel, Georg. *On Individuality and Social Forms.* Chicago: University of Chicago Press, 1972.

Singer, Brian. "The Early Castoriadis: Socialism, Barbarism and the Bureaucratic Thread." *Canadian Journal of Political and Social Theory* 3, no. 3 (1979): 35–56. https://journals.uvic.ca/index.php/ctheory/article/view/13829.

Sitrin, Marina, and Dario Azzelini. *Occupying Language: The Secret Rendezvous with History and the Present.* Brooklyn: Zuccotti Park, 2012.

Smethurst, James. "Black Arts Movement." In *Keywords for African American Studies,* edited by Erica R. Edwards, Roderick A. Ferguson, and Jeffrey O.G. Ogbar, 19–22. New York: NYU Press, 2018.

Smith, Jeremy C.A. "Capitalism." In *Cornelius Castoriadis: Key Concepts,* edited by Suzi Adams, 155–66. London: Bloomsbury, 2014.

Smith, Melissa. "MOMA's Budget Is About the Same Size as the Budget of 150 Museums in 1989 Combined." *Quartz,* May 24, 2014. https://qz.com/207299/momas-endowment-is-about-the-same-size-as-the-budget-of-150-museums-in-1989-combined/.

Straume, Ingerid. "Paidea." In *Cornelius Castoriadis: Key Concepts,* edited by Suzi Adams, 143–54. London: Bloomsbury, 2014.

Taussig, Michael. "I'm So Angry I Made A Sign." In W.J.T. Mitchell, Bernard E. Harcourt, and Michael Taussig, *Occupy: Three Inquiries in Disobedience,* 45–92. Chicago: University of Chicago Press, 2013.

"The Combahee River Collective Statement (1977)." *Black Past.* https://www.blackpast.org/african-american-history/combahee-river-collective-statement-1977/.

"The Introduction from *After the Fall: Communiqués from Occupied California.*" *libcom,* February 16, 2010. https://libcom.org/library/introduction-after-fall-communiqu%C3%A9s-occupied-california.

The Invisible Committee. *Now.* Translated by Robert Hurley. South Pasadena: Semiotext(e), 2017.

———. *The Coming Insurrection.* Los Angeles: Semiotext(e), 2009.

———. *To Our Friends.* Translated by Robert Hurley. South Pasadena: Semiotext(e), 2015.

Thompson, Nato. "Living as Form." In *Living as Form: Socially Engaged Art From 1991–2011,* edited by Nato Thompson, 16–33. New York: Creative Time, 2012.

———. "The Occupation of Wall Street Across Time and Space." *Transversal Texts,* October 2011. https://transversal.at/transversal/1011/thompson/en.

[Tiqqn/Invisible Committee]. "The Call." *Anarchist Library.* https://theanarchistlibrary.org/library/anonymous-call.

Touré, Asia. "Poetry and Black Liberations: Freedom's Furious Passions (Reminiscences)." In *SOS–Calling All Black People: A Black Arts Movement Reader,* edited by John H. Bracey Jr., Sonia Sanchez, and James Smethurst, 25–30. Amherst: University of Massachusetts Press, 2014.

Tuck, Eve, and K. Wayne Yang. "Decolonization Is Not a Metaphor." *Decolonization: Indigeneity, Education and Society* 1, no. 1 (2012): 1–40. https://jps.library.utoronto.ca/index.php/des/article/view/18630.

Ury, William. "Gang Warfare: Mothers as Thirdsiders." *The Third Side*. https://thirdside.williamury.com/mothers-as-thirdsiders/.

Wagley, Catherine G. "Good-Bye to All That: Boyle Heights, Hotbed of Gentrification Protests, Sees Galleries Depart." *ARTnews*, June 8, 2018. http://www.artnews.com/2018/06/08/good-bye-boyle-heights-hotbed-gentrification-protests-sees-galleries-depart/.

Weber, Jasmine. "W.A.G.E. Asks Artists to Demand Payment and Withhold Content from 2019 Whitney Biennial." *Hyperallergic*, January 23, 2019. https://hyperallergic.com/481246/w-a-g-e-asks-artists-to-demand-payment-and-withhold-content-from-2019-whitney-biennial.

———. "Whitney Museum Director Pens Letter After Vice Chair's Relationship to Weapons Manufacturer Is Publicized." *Hyperallergic*, December 3, 2018. https://hyperallergic.com/474176/whitney-museum-director-pens-letter-after-vice-chairs-relationship-to-weapons-manufacturer-is-publicized.

Wilding, Faith. "Written in the Sand: Letter to (Young) Women Artist and Art Historians." In *re:tracing the feminist art program*, ed. Ulrike Muller. http://www.encore.at/retracing/index2.html.

Williams, Raymond. *Marxism and Literature*. Oxford: Oxford University Press, 1977.

Wright, Stephen. *Storming Heaven: Class Composition and Struggle in Italian Autonomist Marxism*. London: Pluto, 2002.